Presidents Trivia Challenge

George Washington through Donald Trump

Cheryl Pryor

Arlington & Amelia Publishers

ISBN-13: 978-1886541313

ISBN-10: 1886541310

FOR

PERRY

TABLE OF CONTENTS

Other Books by Cheryl Pryor

Chosen

Children Of The Presidents

Presidents, First Ladies, & First Family Trivia

The Big Book of Presidential Trivia

The Big Book of First Ladies Trivia

First Family Trivia

American Revolution & The Birth of A Nation Trivia

Living The Word of God

Pregnancy Journal

Precious Moments

Treasured Moments of My Child

My Mother's Life Story

My Father's Life Story

How Much Do You *Really* Know About The Love Of Your Life?

Couples Game Night Challenge

Wedding Survival Guide

Write Now

Legacy

Children's Books

My Child's Keepsake Journal

Trivia For Kids: The Presidents

Trivia For Kids: First Ladies

From the series: The Sullivan Family Series

Savannah In The Big Move

Savannah On Stage

Savannah On Horseback

Savannah in Look What Followed Me Home

Savannah & The Grumpy Neighbor

Savannah & The Mad Scientist

From the series: Savannah's World Travels Series

Savannah's Disney World Celebration

Savannah Goes To Paris

Presidents & First Ladies
& Their Years In Office

Some presidents have been married more than once, but only the wives that were First Ladies are listed. Some wives however that were deceased previous to their husband's presidency are listed, as they are noted posthumously as First Ladies.

1. George Washington / Martha Dandridge Custis Washington 1789 – 1797

2. John Adams / Abigail Smith Adams 1797 – 1801

3. Thomas Jefferson / Martha Wayles Skelton Jefferson (deceased) 1801 – 1809

4. James Madison / Dolley Payne Todd Madison 1809 – 1817

5. James Monroe / Elizabeth Kortright Monroe 1817 – 1825

6. John Quincy Adams / Louisa Catherine Johnson Adams 1825 – 1829

7. Andrew Jackson / Rachel Donelson Jackson (deceased) 1829 – 1837

8. Martin Van Buren / Hannah Hoes Van Buren (deceased) 1837 – 1841

9. William Henry Harrison / Anna Tuthill Symmes Harrison 1841 – 1841

10. John Tyler / Letitia Christian Tyler (1st wife died during his presidency) Julia Gardiner Tyler (2nd wife he married during his presidency) 1841 – 1845

11. James Polk / Sarah Childress Polk 1845 – 1849

12. Zachary Taylor / Margaret "Peggy" Mackall Smith Taylor 1849 – 1850

13. Millard Fillmore / Abigail Powers Fillmore 1850 – 1853

14. Franklin Pierce / Jane Means Appleton Pierce   1853 – 1857

15. James Buchanan / Harriet Lane (niece of James Buchanan) 1857 – 1861

16. Abraham Lincoln / Mary Todd Lincoln 1861 – 1865

17. Andrew Johnson / Eliza McCardle Johnson 1865 – 1869

18. Ulysses S. Grant / Julia Dent Grant 1869 – 1877

19. Rutherford B. Hayes / Lucy Ware Webb Hayes 1877 – 1881

20. James Garfield / Lucretia Rudolph Garfield 1881 – 1881

21. Chester Arthur / Ellen Lewis Herndon Arthur 1881 – 1885

22. Grover Cleveland / Frances Folsom Cleveland 1885 – 1889

23. Benjamin Harrison / Caroline Lavinia Scott Harrison 1889 – 1893

24. Grover Cleveland / Frances Folsom Cleveland 1893 – 1897

25. William McKinley / Ida Saxton McKinley 1897 – 1901

26. Theodore Roosevelt / Edith Kermit Carow Roosevelt (2nd wife) 1901 – 1909

27. William H. Taft / Helen "Nellie" Herron Taft 1909 – 1913

28. Woodrow Wilson / Ellen Axson Wilson (1st wife- died during his presidency)
Edith Bolling Galt Wilson (2nd wife – married during presidency) 1913 –   1921

29. Warren Harding / Florence Kling Harding 1921 – 1923

30. Calvin Coolidge / Grace Anna Goodhue Coolidge 1923 – 1929

31. Herbert Hoover / Lou Henry Hoover 1929 – 1933

32. Franklin D. Roosevelt / Anna "Eleanor" Roosevelt (her maiden name was also Roosevelt) Roosevelt 1933 – 1945

33. Harry Truman / Elizabeth "Bess" Virginia Wallace Truman 1945 – 1953

34. Dwight D. Eisenhower / Mamie Geneva Doud Eisenhower 1953 – 1961

35. John F. Kennedy / Jacqueline "Jackie" Lee Bouvier Kennedy 1961 – 1963

36. Lyndon B. Johnson / Claudia "Lady Bird" Taylor Johnson 1963 – 1969

37. Richard Nixon / Patricia "Pat" Ryan Nixon 1969 – 1974

38. Gerald Ford / Elizabeth "Betty" Bloomer Ford 1974 – 1977

39. Jimmy Carter / Rosalynn Smith Carter 1977 – 1981

40. Ronald Reagan / Nancy Davis Reagan (2nd wife) 1981 – 1989

41. George H.W. Bush / Barbara Pierce Bush 1989 – 1993

42. Bill Clinton / Hillary Rodham Clinton 1993 – 2001

43. George W. Bush / Laura Welch Bush 2001 – 2009

44. Barack Obama / Michelle LaVaughn Robinson Obama 2009 – 2017

45. Donald Trump / Melania Knavs Trump (3rd wife)   2017 - ?

1

Test Your Presidential Knowledge

Answers are given on pages 7 - 8.

1. Which president gave up horseback riding and instead took up riding a mechanical horse?

A. Calvin Coolidge   *C. Lyndon B. Johnson*

B. George W. Bush   *D. Grover Cleveland*

2. Which president stated he had seen a UFO?

A. George W. Bush   *C. Jimmy Carter*

B. Dwight D. Eisenhower   *D. Ronald Reagan*

3. Which president was blind in one eye from a boxing match he was in?

A. Lyndon B. Johnson   *C. Gerald Ford*

B. Grover Cleveland   *D. Theodore Roosevelt*

4. Who is the only president in the twentieth century to not have a college degree?

A. Harry Truman   *C. Barack Obama*

B. *Lyndon B. Johnson*   D. *Donald Trump*

5. At one time which president was an owner of the Texas Rangers baseball team?

A. *Gerald Ford*   C. *George H.W. Bush*

B. *Lyndon B. Johnson*   D. *George W. Bush*

6. Which president worked as a fashion model?

A. *Gerald Ford*   C. *John F. Kennedy*

B. *Ronald Reagan*   D. *Bill Clinton*

7. Which president was a skilled chef?

A. *George H.W. Bush*   C. *Calvin Coolidge*

B. *William McKinley*   D. *Dwight D. Eisenhower*

8. Which two presidents were married to foreign born First Ladies?

A. *J. Adams & J.F. Kennedy*   C. *J. Monroe & D. Trump*

B. *W. McKinley & M. Van Buren*   D. *J.Q. Adams & D. Trump*

9. Who is the only president to have been a professional actor?

A. *Gerald Ford*   C. *Warren Harding*

B. *Ronald Reagan*   D. *Donald Trump*

10. Which president played the saxophone?

A. Bill Clinton

C. Warren Harding

B. Gerald Ford

D. James Buchanan

11. Which president is the only president whose first language was not English?

A. Rutherford B. Hayes

C. Ulysses S. Grant

B. Martin Van Buren

D. James Monroe

12. Which president was a mimic and loved to tell dialect jokes in English, Irish, and Scottish accents?

A. Woodrow Wilson

C. Theodore Roosevelt

B. Lyndon B. Johnson

D. George W. Bush

13. What president loved to paint for relaxation? He couldn't draw so someone else would sketch the picture and he would paint it.

A. Woodrow Wilson

C. Dwight D. Eisenhower

B. George W. Bush

D. William H. Taft

14. Who was the only president to earn a doctorate?

A. Woodrow Wilson

C. Harry Truman

B. Bill Clinton

D. Calvin Coolidge

15. What president collected comic books?

A. George W. Bush   C. Bill Clinton

B. Barack Obama   D. Donald Trump

16. Which president painted his golf balls black in the winter so he could see them in the snow?

A. Woodrow Wilson   C. Dwight D. Eisenhower

B. George H.W. Bush   D. Barack Obama

17. Who was the only bachelor to be president in American history?

A. Thomas Jefferson   C. James Buchanan

B. Martin Van Buren   D. John Tyler

18. Which president was captain of Yale University's baseball team?

A. George W. Bush   C. Ronald Reagan

B. Gerald Ford   D. George H.W. Bush

19. Which future president had the job of scrubbing toilets while in the navy?

A. Jimmy Carter   C. George W. Bush

B. Richard Nixon   D. Lyndon B. Johnson

20. It's a well-known fact that many of our presidents have loved to play golf, but can you name which president actually owned seventeen golf courses at the time of his presidency?

A. George H.W. Bush   C. Donald Trump

B. Dwight D. Eisenhower   D. John F. Kennedy

21. During his college days, which president was Most Valuable Player and was offered a football career by the Green Bay Packers and the Detroit Lions?

A. George H.W. Bush   C. Gerald Ford

B. William H. Taft   D. Theodore Roosevelt

22. Many former presidents have been interviewed on late night talk shows and asked about aliens and Area 51. Which president admitted when the 50th anniversary of the alleged UFO crash in Roswell was coming up, he had his aides look into if there were aliens at Area 51?

A. Dwight D. Eisenhower   C. George W. Bush

B. Jimmy Carter   D. Bill Clinton

23. Who was the only president to weigh under one hundred pounds?

A. William H. Taft   C. James Madison

B. Millard Fillmore   D. Franklin Pierce

24. Which president, receiving his wings at the age of nineteen, was the nation's youngest commissioned pilot?

A. George W. Bush   C. Dwight D. Eisenhower

B. Jimmy Carter   D. George H.W. Bush

25. Which president never voted until he was sixty-two years of age?

A. Donald Trump

C. Thomas Jefferson

B. Ulysses S. Grant

D. Zachary Taylor

Answers

Chapter 1 – Test Your Presidential Knowledge

1. A - Calvin Coolidge

2. C - Jimmy Carter

3. D - Theodore Roosevelt

4. A - Harry Truman

5. D - George W. Bush

6. A -Gerald Ford

During his days at Yale he had invested in a modeling agency. He posed for ski-wear ads.

7. D - Dwight D. Eisenhower

8. D - John Quincy Adams & Donald Trump

9. B - Ronald Reagan

His first wife, Jane Wyman, who he was divorced from was a well-known actress also. His second wife, First Lady Nancy Reagan, was a lesser known actress.

10. A - Bill Clinton

11. B – Martin Van Buren

His first language was Dutch.

12. A - Woodrow Wilson

13. C - Dwight D. Eisenhower

14. A - Woodrow Wilson

15. B - Barack Obama

16. A - Woodrow Wilson

17. C - James Buchanan

Grover Cleveland was a bachelor when he was elected but was married during his first administration.

18. D - George H.W. Bush

19. A - Jimmy Carter

20. C - Donald Trump

21. C - Gerald Ford

22. D - Bill Clinton

23. C - James Madison

He was 5'4 and weighed ninety-eight pounds.

24. D - George H.W. Bush

25. C - Zachary Taylor

2

Home States Of Our Presidents

Answers are given on page 12.

1. Which state is able to claim the fact that the majority of the presidents claimed it as their home state?

    A. Ohio   *C. Tennessee*

    B. Virginia   *D. New York*

2. Which state has produced 7 presidents?

    A. Virginia   *C. Massachusetts*

    B. New York   *D. Ohio*

3. How many states can lay claim to having a president from their state?

    A. 7   *C. 11*

    B. 5   *D. 18*

4. Before Donald Trump, who was the last president to have come from New York?

    A. Grover Cleveland   *C. Franklin D Roosevelt*

    B. Harry Truman   *D. Warren Harding*

5. Who was the last president to come from the deep south?

    A. Andrew Johnson   *C. Ulysses S. Grant*

    B .Jimmy Carter   *D. William Henry Harrison*

6. Which president was said to be born in Hawaii, the only president to have been born away from the continental U.S.?

    A. Barack Obama   *C. Gerald Ford*

    B. Donald Trump   *D. Martin Van Buren*

7. Four presidents lay claim to their home state being Massachusetts. Can you name the four presidents?

    A. John Adams, John Quincy Adams, Calvin Coolidge, John F. Kennedy

    B. John Adams. James Madison, John Quincy Adams, John F. Kennedy

    C. James Polk, Millard Fillmore, Franklin Pierce, John F. Kennedy

    D. W. H. Harrison, James Buchanan, William McKinley, John F. Kennedy

8. Four of the eight presidents who died in office came from what state?

    A. New York   *C. Ohio*

    B. Virginia   *D. Tennessee*

9. When George Washington completed his second administration of the presidency he returned to his home Mount Vernon, which is in what state?

    A. Massachusetts   *C. Rhode Island*

    B. Virginia   *D. New York*

10. What state is our current president from?

    A. New York   *C. Ohio*

    B. Kentucky   *D. Florida*

Answers

Chapter 2 – Home States Of Our Presidents

1. B - Virginia

8 presidents have come from Virginia. 4 out of 5 of the founding fathers who later became presidents came from Virginia. They were: Washington, Jefferson, Madison, and Monroe. Virginia was the wealthiest and most populous state in our nation's earliest days which helps explains why so many of the young nation's first few leaders came from there.

2. D – Ohio

The presidents from Ohio are: Ulysses S. Grant, Rutherford B. Hayes , James A. Garfield, Benjamin Harrison, William McKinley, William Howard Taft, and Warren Harding

3. D - 18

4. C – Franklin D. Roosevelt

5. B – Jimmy Carter who was from Georgia

6. A – Barack Obama

7. A - John Adams, John Quincy Adams, Calvin Coolidge, John F. Kennedy

8. C - Ohio

9. B – Virginia

10. A. New York

As of the time this book was printed that would be Donald Trump who is from New York

3

On The Campaign Trail & Nail Biting Elections

Answers are given on page 16.

1. Which president, while campaigning for the presidency made the statement that he had campaigned in fifty-seven states with one state left to go?

A. George W. Bush

C. Jimmy Carter

B. Barack Obama

D. Bill Clinton

2. Who was the only president elected by a unanimous electoral vote?

A. George Washington

C. Thomas Jefferson

B. John Adams

D. Franklin D. Roosevelt

3. Who was also running on the ballot for America's first president other than George Washington?

A. John Adams

C. Alexander Hamilton

B. Thomas Jefferson

D. Samuel Adams

4. Which president's campaign was not only entertaining but shocking and controversial where he, a billionaire businessman and real estate magnate and *not* a politician, stunned the establishment when he beat all seventeen of his primary opponents and went on to win the presidency to win against his Democratic nominee who was considered a shoo-in for the win?

    A. Abraham Lincoln   *C. Herbert Hoover*

    B. John F. Kennedy   *D. Donald Trump*

5. Which president helped fund his first political campaign from money he won playing poker while in the Navy?

    A. Jimmy Carter   *C. Richard Nixon*

    B. George H.W. Bush   *D. Dwight D. Eisenhower*

6. Expecting to lose the election after the first returns came in, what president went to bed thinking he had lost the election? He ended up winning the election with the final count being 185 to 184.

    A. Harry Truman   *C. Warren Harding*

    B. John Tyler   *D. Rutherford B. Hayes*

7. When this president ran for a second term he received 525 out of 538 electoral votes and carried 49 out of 50 states – *the largest number ever won*. Who was he?

    A. George Washington   *C. Thomas Jefferson*

    B. John F. Kennedy   *D. Ronald Reagan*

8. Which president during his campaign threatened to "lock her up" referring to his opponent a former first lady?

A. Barack Obama

C. Donald Trump

B. George W. Bush

D. Bill Clinton

9. Which president won the Electoral College vote in one of the closest and most controversial elections in America's history? It took over a month of recounts from Florida's voters before the winner was announced. He was declared president, even though his opponent had more popular votes.

A. Donald Trump

C. Ronald Reagan

B. George W. Bush

D. Richard Nixon

10. Which president won his presidential election by 61% of the popular vote, the largest margin of victory in history?

A. Lyndon B. Johnson

C. Ronald Reagan

B. John F. Kennedy

D. Bill Clinton

Answers

Chapter 3 – On The Campaign Trail & Nail Biting Elections

1. B - Barack Obama

That's right, he said fifty-seven states with one left to go.

2. A - George Washington

3. A - John Adams

4. D - Donald Trump

5. C - Richard Nixon

6. D - Rutherford B. Hayes

7. D - Ronald Reagan

8. C - Donald Trump

9. B - George W. Bush

10. A - Lyndon B. Johnson

4

Which President Am I?

Answers are given on pages 25 - 27.

1. The terrorist bombing at the Boston Marathon occurred during his presidency.

A. Bill Clinton   *C. George W. Bush*

B. Barack Obama   *D. Donald Trump*

2. His time of presidency was termed the "Era of Good Feelings." Which president was he?

A. George Washington   *C. James Monroe*

B. Abraham Lincoln   *D. Ronald Reagan*

3. The collapse of communism in the Soviet Union occurred while he was president.

A. Ronald Reagan   *C. Harry Truman*

B. George H. W. Bush   *D. Bill Clinton*

4. Which president was the only president to resign?

A. William Henry Harrison   *C. Grover Cleveland*

B. Ulysses S. Grant   *D. Richard Nixon*

5. Who was the first president to be assassinated?

A. Abraham Lincoln   C. John F. Kennedy

B. James Garfield   D. William McKinley

6. Which president could write Greek with one hand while writing Latin with the other hand at the same time?

A. Rutherford B. Hayes   C. Chester Arthur

B. James Garfield   D. Franklin D. Roosevelt

7. He was president during the covert operation that led to the killing of Osama bin Laden.

A. George H.W. Bush   C. George W. Bush

B. Bill Clinton   D. Barack Obama

8. Which president was fluent in seven languages?

A. John Quincy Adams   C. Woodrow Wilson

B. William H. Taft   D. Warren Harding

9. The beginning of America's worst financial crisis since the Great Depression began during his presidency. Which president was it?

A. Franklin D. Roosevelt   C. Herbert Hoover

B. Jimmy Carter   D. George W. Bush

10. The stock market crash (of 1929) happened during whose presidency

which brought about the Great Depression?

A. Andrew Johnson

C. William H. Taft

B. Herbert Hoover

D. Franklin D. Roosevelt

11. Which president served on the First Continental Congress and helped draft the Declaration of Independence? He was a vice-president and a president. He earned a master's degree at Harvard. He was a patriot. He represented the British soldiers who were on trial for the Boston Massacre; even though others resented his decision to do so, he did this because of his strong belief that every person deserves a defense.

A. George Washington

C. Thomas Jefferson

B. John Adams

D. James Monroe

12. Who was president at the time suicide bombers killed over two hundred Americans when they attacked the Marine barracks in Beirut?

A. Ronald Reagan

C. George H. W. Bush

B. George W. Bush

D. Bill Clinton

13. Which president introduced the Bill of Rights and the first ten Amendments to the Constitution?

A. John Adams

C. Thomas Jefferson

B. James Madison

D. John Quincy Adams

14. Which president from the moment he took the oath of office was threatened by the left of impeachment? One reason given is they stated he colluded with the Russian government to meddle with the U.S.'s

presidential election, even though there has been no evidence of him having done so?

A. Lyndon B. Johnson

C. Donald Trump

B. John F. Kennedy

D. Bill Clinton

15. Which president was the only twentieth century president who did not attend college?

A. Barack Obama

C. Ronald Reagan

B. Lyndon B. Johnson

D. Harry Truman

16. Which president killed a man in a duel who dishonored his wife?

A. Martin Van Buren

C. James Polk

B. James Garfield

D. Andrew Jackson

17. There was a great bit of controversy over where this president was born and if he was even eligible to be president. This was called the birther controversy. Who was the president?

A. Barack Obama

C. John Quincy Adams

B. Dwight D. Eisenhower

D. Chester Arthur

18. After being vice-president for only three months and after only meeting with the president a few times he became president himself. Do you know who he is?

A. Andrew Johnson

C. Theodore Roosevelt

B. Chester Arthur

D. Harry Truman

19. Who was president during the 9/11 terrorist attacks?

A. Barack Obama   C. Jimmy Carter

B. George W. Bush   D. Bill Clinton

20. Which president was the grandson of the 9th president and also became president himself?

A. John Quincy Adams   C. Lyndon B. Johnson

B. George H.W. Bush   D. Benjamin Harrison

21. While he was president there was no vice-president.

A. George Washington   C. Chester Arthur

B. Andrew Johnson   D. Lyndon B. Johnson

22. In the final year of his presidency the stock market plunged and the housing and banking industries were in a mess. Who was he?

A. George W. Bush   C. Jimmy Carter

B. Franklin D. Roosevelt   D. Herbert Hoover

23. Which president was a direct descendant of William Brewster, the Pilgrim leader who arrived on the Mayflower?

A. Zachary Taylor   C. John Adams

B Franklin Pierce   D. William McKinley

24. Which president was the son of Irish immigrants?

A. *Martin Van Buren*   C. *Millard Fillmore*

B. *Andrew Jackson*   D. *John F. Kennedy*

25. Which president banished alcohol from the White House?

A. *Ulysses S. Grant*   C. *James Buchanan*

B. *Woodrow Wilson*   D. *Rutherford B. Hayes*

26. Who was president when the '*Star Spangled Banner*' became our national anthem?

A. *Herbert Hoover*   C. *Franklin Pierce*

B. *Abraham Lincoln*   D. *Chester Arthur*

27. Which president believed the president was 'a steward to the people' and that it was his place to take action for the good of the public?

A. *Abraham Lincoln*   C. *Theodore Roosevelt*

B. *Franklin D. Roosevelt*   D. *Jimmy Carter*

28. After promising no new taxes in his presidential campaign which president lost the support of many people when he did indeed raise tax revenues?

A. *George H.W. Bush*   C. *Barack Obama*

B. *Richard Nixon*   D. *Harry Truman*

29. His second term as president began with the worst financial crisis in U.S. History.

A. *Franklin D. Roosevelt*   C. *Herbert Hoover*

B. *Grover Cleveland*   D. *Barack Obama*

30. Which two presidents were impeached by Congress, but not removed from office?

A. *R. Nixon & B. Clinton*   C. *A. Johnson & R. Nixon*

B. *A. Johnson & B. Clinton*   D. *R. Nixon & D. Trump*

31. Included in which president's library is a graffiti covered section of the Berlin Wall donated to him by the people of Berlin?

A. *Franklin D. Roosevelt*   C. *Harry Truman*

B. *Dwight D. Eisenhower*   D. *Ronald Reagan*

32. Which president spoke to the public on the radio which were called "Fireside Chats?"

A. *Theodore Roosevelt*   C. *Warren Harding*

B. *Calvin Coolidge*   D. *Franklin D. Roosevelt*

33. During his presidency the U.S. enjoyed peace and economic well-being, more so than at any other time in history. Who was he?

A. *Bill Clinton*   C. *Barack Obama*

B. *Ronald Reagan*   D. *Richard Nixon*

34. He was one of the American diplomats sent to negotiate the Treaty of Paris which ended the Revolutionary War and recognized American

independence. Which president is he?

    A. John Adams   *C. John Quincy Adams*

    B. Thomas Jefferson   *D. James Madison*

35. Which president was originally a liberal Democrat but ran for the presidency as a conservative Republican?

    A. Barack Obama   *C. Ronald Reagan*

    B. Benjamin Harrison   *D. Abraham Lincoln*

Answers

Chapter 4 - Which President Am I

1. B - Barack Obama

2. C - James Monroe

3. B - George H.W. Bush

4. D - Richard Nixon

5. A - Abraham Lincoln

6. B - James Garfield

7. D - Barack Obama

8. A - John Quincy Adams

9. D - George W. Bush

10. B - Herbert Hoover

11. B - John Adams

12. A - Ronald Reagan

13. B - James Madison

14. C - Donald Trump

15. D - Harry Truman

16. D - Andrew Jackson

17. A – Barack Obama

18. D - Harry Truman

19. B - George W. Bush

20. D - Benjamin Harrison

21. C - Chester Arthur

President Arthur assumed office at the death of President Garfield. Arthur requested a Senate special session. to ensure that the Senate had legal authority to convene immediately and choose a Senate president pro tempore, who would be able to assume the presidency if Arthur himself died during his administration.

22. A - George W. Bush

23. A - Zachary Taylor

24. B - Andrew Jackson

25. D - Rutherford B. Hayes

26. A - Herbert Hoover

27. C - Theodore Roosevelt

28. A - George H.W. Bush

29. B - Grover Cleveland

30. B - Andrew Johnson, Bill Clinton

Richard Nixon resigned before he could be impeached, so you can't count him.

31. D - Ronald Reagan

32. D - Franklin D. Roosevelt

33. A - Bill Clinton

34. A or B - John Adams or Thomas Jefferson, either or both is correct

The Treaty of Paris negotiated between the colonies and Great Britain

ended the Revolutionary War and recognized American independence. Five men had been commissioned to negotiate the treaty. These men were: John Adams, Ben Franklin, John Jay, Thomas Jefferson, and Henry Laurens. The negotiations were completed by John Adams, Ben Franklin, and John Jay. Henry Laurens had been captured en route by the British and Thomas Jefferson left the colonies too late to be a part of the negotiations.

35. C - Ronald Reagan

5

Before And After Their Days In The White House

Answers are given on pages 34 - 35.

1. Which president was a U.S. Minister to the Netherlands during one presidential administration, minister to Prussia during a different administration, and ambassador to the Russian court of Czar Alexander I during yet another administration, and then off to Great Britain, all before becoming president himself?

    A. John Quincy Adams   *C. James Madison*

    B. Thomas Jefferson   *D. Rutherford B. Hayes*

2. Which president in the days before his presidency was a reality TV star?

    A. Ronald Reagan   *C. Donald Trump*

    B. Gerald Ford   *D. George W. Bush*

3. Which president was also a Founding Father, a vice-president to another president, and had a son who would also become president, and was also a descendant of Puritan colonists?

A. James Madison   C. John Adams

B. Thomas Jefferson   D. James Monroe

4. Who was the only American president to have headed two branches of government – executive and judicial?

A. William McKinley   C. Woodrow Wilson

B. William Howard Taft   D. Rutherford B. Hayes

5. Which president was an inventor, and many of his inventions can be seen at his home today which is open to visitors?

A. Herbert Hoover   C. Calvin Coolidge

B. James Garfield   D. Thomas Jefferson

6. Which president wrote nine of the ten amendments known as the Bill of Rights?

A. Thomas Jefferson   C. James Monroe

B. James Madison   D. John Quincy Adams

7. Who were the only two signers of the Declaration of Independence to become president?

A. Washington & Jefferson   C. Washington & Adams

B. Adams & Jefferson   D. Jefferson & Madison

8. He was in China during the Boxer Rebellion where he organized help

for foreigners and years later when WWI began he helped Americans who were in Europe. This humanitarian, years later would also help Belgians after the intrusion of German troops. Who was he?

A. John Quincy Adams

C. James Buchanan

B. William H. Taft

D. Herbert Hoover

9. Which president, after retirement, penned his memoirs while suffering from throat cancer so his wife would be financially stable?

A. Ulysses S. Grant

C. John Adams

B. Zachary Taylor

D. Franklin D. Roosevelt

10. As a delegate to the Constitutional Convention in 1787, which president earned the title 'Father of the Constitution'?

A. Thomas Jefferson

C. George Washington

B. James Monroe

D. James Madison

11. Which president was an actor before he was president?

A. Ronald Reagan

C. George W. Bush

B. John F. Kennedy

D. Donald Trump

12. Before he became president he was promoted to general of the army. He was the first commander since George Washington to hold that rank. Who was he?

A. Dwight D. Eisenhower

C. Ulysses S. Grant

B. Zachary Taylor

D. Andrew Jackson

13. He studied law under Thomas Jefferson who would become his mentor. Who was he?

    A. John Quincy Adams   C. John Tyler

    B. James Monroe   D. Franklin Pierce

14. He was the author of the Declaration of Independence. Who was he?

    A. Thomas Jefferson   C. James Madison

    B. John Adams   D. James Monroe

15. Before he became president he served in the navy. His boat was rammed and he swam to safety and towed an injured man by his life jacket strap with his teeth. He scratched a message on a coconut shell to insure their rescue. Who was he?

    A. George H.W. Bush   C. Richard Nixon

    B. John F. Kennedy   D. Jimmy Carter

16. Which president worked as a cattle rancher?

    A. Ronald Reagan   C. Grover Cleveland

    B. Gerald Ford   D. Theodore Roosevelt

17. He, along with the U.S. minister to France, actually approved and signed the Louisiana Purchase agreement. Who was he?

    A. Thomas Jefferson   C. James Monroe

    B. James Madison   D. John Adams

18. Which president was victim to a Wall Street scam leaving him and his wife in financial ruin?

A. Donald Trump   *C. George H.W. Bush*

B. Rutherford B. Hayes   *D. Ulysses S. Grant*

19. He was the only five star general to become president. Who was he?

A. George Washington   *C. Theodore Roosevelt*

B. William Henry Harrison   *D. Dwight D. Eisenhower*

20. At one time he had to resort to selling firewood on the street to support his family. Who was he?

A. Abraham Lincoln   *C. John Tyler*

B. Ulysses S. Grant   *D. Zachary Taylor*

21. Which former president has been accused of being involved in a "pay-to-play" scheme in which foreign governments could donate money to his foundation in exchange for beneficial treatment from the government influenced by the former president and former first lady who at the time was the Secretary of State?

A. Barack Obama   *C. Bill Clinton*

B. Richard Nixon   *D. George H.W. Bush*

22. Which president, after he retired, went on an African safari and brought back plant samples and animals for the Smithsonian?

A. Theodore Roosevelt   *C. Ulysses S. Grant*

B. *Chester Arthur*   D. *Grover Cleveland*

23. Which president was a school teacher before he was president?

A. *Millard Fillmore*   C. *Andrew Johnson*

B. *Lyndon B. Johnson*   D. *Harry Truman*

24. Which president made a major contribution to the ratification of the Constitution by writing The Federalist Papers?

A. *James Madison*   C. *Thomas Jefferson*

B. *John Adams*   D. *John Quincy Adams*

25. An Indian chieftain, Tecumseh, began an Indian confederation to prevent settlers from coming in and taking more of their land. This future president's troops killed Tecumseh and afterward the Indians scattered, no longer causing a serious threat. Who was he?

A. *Andrew Johnson*   C. *Andrew Jackson*

B. *Zachary Taylor*   D. *William Henry Harrison*

Answers

Chapter 5 - Before And After Their Days In The White House

1. A - John Quincy Adams

2. C - Donald Trump

3. C - John Adams

4. B - William Howard Taft

5. D - Thomas Jefferson

6. B - James Madison

7. B - John Adams & Thomas Jefferson

8. D - Herbert Hoover

9. A - Ulysses S. Grant

10. D - James Madison

11. A - Ronald Reagan

*While technically you could also say Donald Trump was an actor as he acted in one movie which was a flop and he also starred in a reality show, Ronald Reagan was a professional actor acting in over a dozen movies.

12. C- Ulysses S. Grant

13. B - James Monroe

14. A - Thomas Jefferson

15. B - John F. Kennedy

16. D - Theodore Roosevelt

17. C- James Monroe

He was sent to France by President Thomas Jefferson to help negotiate the sale of the Port of Orleans. Once arriving in France Monroe learned that Napoleon Bonaparte, to help finance his war in Europe, was willing to sell the entire Louisiana Territory. Not having time to seek presidential approval Monroe and Livingston (U.S. Minister to France) signed the agreement themselves. This doubled the size of the U.S.

18. D - Ulysses S. Grant

19. D - Dwight D. Eisenhower

He retired to a home overlooking the battlefield at Gettysburg, Pennsylvania.

20. B - Ulysses S. Grant

21. C - Bill Clinton

22. A - Theodore Roosevelt

23. B - Lyndon B. Johnson

24. A - James Madison

25. D. William Henry Harrison

Tecumseh was a Shawnee leader.

6

Historical Times Of Our Nation

Answers are given on pages 42 - 43.

1. Who was president when 9/11 occurred?

    A. George H.W. Bush   *C. George W. Bush*

    B. Bill Clinton   *D. Barack Obama*

2. Who was president when Apollo 11 landed on the moon in 1969?

    A. John F. Kennedy   *C. Richard Nixon*

    B. Lyndon B. Johnson   *D. Gerald Ford*

3. Who was president when the first atomic bombs were dropped in Hiroshima and Nagasaki in the year 1945?

    A. Franklin D. Roosevelt   *C. Herbert Hoover*

    B. Harry Truman   *D. Dwight D. Eisenhower*

4. Who was president at the start of the California Gold Rush?

    A. James Polk   *C. Millard Fillmore*

B. *John Tyler*   D. *James Buchanan*

5. Who was president during the war of 1812?

   A. *John Adams*   C. *Thomas Jefferson*

   B. *James Madison*   D. *James Monroe*

6. Who was president when Charles Lindbergh flew his solo Transatlantic flight in 1927?

   A. *Calvin Coolidge*   C. *Woodrow Wilson*

   B. *Franklin D. Roosevelt*   D. *William McKinley*

7. Who was president in 1861 when Civil War broke out?

   A. *Franklin Pierce*   C. *Ulysses S. Grant*

   B. *James Buchanan*   D. *Abraham Lincoln*

8. Who was president when Wilbur and Orville Wright first flew in 1903?

   A. *Theodore Roosevelt*   C. *James Garfield*

   B. *Benjamin Harrison*   D. *William Henry Harrison*

9. Who was president when the Pony Express began?

   A. *Martin Van Buren*   C. *Franklin Pierce*

   B. *Chester Arthur*   D. *James Buchanan*

10. Who was president when the U.S. Purchased Alaska?

    A. Andrew Johnson   *C. Thomas Jefferson*

    B. Woodrow Wilson   *D. Theodore Roosevelt*

11. Who was president when Custer's last stand took place?

    A. William Henry Harrison   *C. Zachary Taylor*

    B. Rutherford B. Hayes   *D. Ulysses S. Grant*

12. Who was president when Japan attacked Pearl Harbor in 1941?

    A. Theodore Roosevelt   *C. Franklin D. Roosevelt*

    B. Woodrow Wilson   *D. Harry Truman*

13. Who was president when we were presented the Statue of Liberty as a gift from France in 1886?

    A. Grover Cleveland   *C. William McKinley*

    B. William H. Taft   *D. Warren Harding*

14. Who was president when, what later became known as the Louisiana Purchase, was acquired by the United States?

    A. Theodore Roosevelt   *C. James Polk*

    B. Thomas Jefferson   *D. James Madison*

15. Who was president when the Trail of Tears, a series of forced relocation of Native American nations in the United States occurred?

A. *Andrew Jackson* C. *Andrew Johnson*

B. *Martin Van Buren* D. *John Tyler*

16. There were 5 presidents during the U.S.'s involvement in the Vietnam War, who were they?

A. *Dwight D. Eisenhower, Harry Truman, John F. Kennedy, Lyndon B. Johnson & Jimmy Carter*

B. *John F. Kennedy, Lyndon B. Johnson, Richard Nixon, Harry Truman, & Dwight D. Eisenhower*

C. *Dwight D. Eisenhower, John F. Kennedy, Lyndon B. Johnson, Richard Nixon, & Gerald Ford*

D. *John F. Kennedy, Lyndon B. Johnson, Richard Nixon, Gerald Ford, & Ronald Reagan*

17. Who was president when the ceremonial gold spike was struck completing the First Transcontinental Railroad across the United States connecting the Central Pacific and Union Pacific railroads in 1869?

A. *Ulysses S. Grant* C. *Rutherford B. Hayes*

B. *James Buchanan* D. *Benjamin Harrison*

18. Who was president when WWI broke out?

A. *William McKinley* C. *Woodrow Wilson*

B. *Rutherford B. Hayes* D. *William H. Taft*

19. Who was president in 1959 when Hawaii became the 50th state?

A. *Dwight D. Eisenhower* C. *Barack Obama*

B. *Calvin Coolidge*   D. *Woodrow Wilson*

20. Who was president when the stock market crashed in 1929?

A. *Franklin D. Roosevelt*   C. *Ulysses S. Grant*

B. *Grover Cleveland*   D. *Herbert Hoover*

21. Who was president during Desert Storm?

A. *Dwight D. Eisenhower*   C. *George H.W. Bush*

B. *Bill Clinton*   D. *George W. Bush*

22. Who was president when the 19th Amendment to the Constitution allowed women to vote?

A. *Woodrow Wilson*   C. *James Buchanan*

B. *Calvin Coolidge*   D. *James Garfield*

23. Who was president when WWII broke out?

A. *Franklin D. Roosevelt*   C. *John F. Kennedy*

B. *Herbert Hoover*   D. *Harry Truman*

24. Who was president when the 13th Amendment abolished slavery?

A. *Andrew Johnson*   C. *Ulysses S. Grant*

B. *James Buchanan*   D. *Abraham Lincoln*

25. Who was president at the time of the anti-communist McCarthyism witch hunt?

A. John F. Kennedy

C. Lyndon B. Johnson

B. Harry Truman

D. Dwight D. Eisenhower

Answers

Chapter 6 - Historical Times Of Our Nation

1. C - George W Bush

2. C - Richard Nixon

3. B - Harry Truman

4. A - James Polk

5. B - James Madison

6. A - Calvin Coolidge

7. D – Abraham Lincoln

* Abraham Lincoln came into office just a few weeks before Civil War broke out.

8. A - Theodore Roosevelt

9. D - James Buchanan

10. A - Andrew Johnson

11. D - Ulysses S. Grant

12. C - Franklin D Roosevelt

13. A - Grover Cleveland

14. B - Thomas Jefferson

15. B – Martin Van Buren

*Andrew Jackson signed the Indian Removal Act but left office before it was implemented. At the time it occurred President Martin Van Buren was in office.

16. C - Dwight D. Eisenhower, John F. Kennedy, Lyndon B. Johnson, Richard Nixon, and Gerald Ford

17. A - Ulysses S. Grant

18. C - Woodrow Wilson

19. A - Dwight D. Eisenhower

20. D - Herbert Hoover

21. C – George H.W. Bush

22. A - Woodrow Wilson

23. A - Franklin D Roosevelt

24. D - Abraham Lincoln

25. B - Harry Truman

7

I Was The First President To...

Answers are given on pages 50 - 52.

1. Who was the first president to die while in office?

   A. Abraham Lincoln

   B. William Henry Harrison

   C. William McKinley

   D. Zachary Taylor

2. Who was the first president with a physical disability?

   A. James Polk

   B. Franklin Pierce

   C. Franklin D. Roosevelt

   D. Woodrow Wilson

3. Who was the first president to live in the White House?

   A. John Adams

   B. Thomas Jefferson

   C. James Madison

   D. George Washington

4. Who was the first president to take the oath of office in Washington, D.C.?

   A. George Washington

   C. Thomas Jefferson

B. *John Adams*   D. *James Madison*

5. Who was the first president to marry while in office?

    A. *James Buchanan*   C. *John Tyler*

    B. *Woodrow Wilson*   D. *James Polk*

6. Who was the first president to have his oath of office administered by a woman?

    A. *Barack Obama*   C. *John F. Kennedy*

    B. *Franklin D. Roosevelt*   D. *Lyndon B. Johnson*

7. Which sitting president was the first to visit the Western Wall in Jerusalem, one of Judaism's holiest sites?

    A. *William McKinley*   C. *William H. Taft*

    B. *Donald Trump*   D. *George H.W. Bush*

8. Who was the first president to travel outside the United States while president?

    A. *Theodore Roosevelt*   C. *James Monroe*

    B. *Herbert Hoover*   D. *Rutherford B. Hayes*

9. While he was president the first telephone was installed in the White House. Who is he?

    A. *Andrew Johnson*   C. *Grover Cleveland*

B. *Rutherford B. Hayes*   D. *James Garfield*

10. Who was the first president to have set eyes on the Pacific Ocean?

   A. *Millard Fillmore*   C. *Benjamin Harrison*

   B. *Ulysses S. Grant*   D. *William H. Taft*

11. Who is the first president, and only to date, to earn a doctorate degree, PhD.?

   A. *Harry Truman*   C. *Barack Obama*

   B. *Bill Clinton*   D. *Woodrow Wilson*

12. Who was the first president (first and only) to have the oath of office administered aboard Air Force One?

   A. *George H.W. Bush*   C. *Lyndon B. Johnson*

   B. *Gerald Ford*   D. *Harry Truman*

13. By the end of his presidency the nation reached from the Atlantic to the Pacific Ocean for the first time. Who is he?

   A. *James Polk*   C. *Martin Van Buren*

   B. *Millard Fillmore*   D. *James Buchanan*

14. Who was the first president to voice support for same-sex marriage?

   A. *Bill Clinton*   C. *Barack Obama*

   B. *George W. Bush*   D. *Jimmy Carter*

15. Who was the first president born in the twentieth century?

A. Dwight D. Eisenhower

B. Gerald Ford

C. George W. Bush

D. John F. Kennedy

16. Who was the first president to be photographed?

A. James Madison

B. Abraham Lincoln

C. Zachary Taylor

D. John Quincy Adams

17. Who won the first presidential race in which women were allowed to vote?

A. Warren Harding

B. Harry Truman

C. Woodrow Wilson

D. Franklin D. Roosevelt

18. Who was the first president to be born in the United States?

A. Andrew Jackson

B. Martin Van Buren

C. Chester Arthur

D. John Tyler

19. Who was the first president licensed to fly a plane?

A. Calvin Coolidge

B. George H.W. Bush

C. Dwight D. Eisenhower

D. Gerald Ford

20. Who was the first president who was not a politician, but a businessman when he became president?

47

A. Herbert Hoover   C. Donald Trump

B. George W. Bush   D. Harry Truman

21. Who was the first president to be impeached, but was acquitted by one vote?

A. Andrew Johnson   C. Richard Nixon

B. Bill Clinton   D. Donald Trump

22. Who was the first African-American president?

A. Warren Harding   C. Chester Arthur

B. Barack Obama   D. Bill Clinton

23. Who was the first president to visit all fifty states?

A. Richard Nixon   C. Dwight D. Eisenhower

B. Bill Clinton   D. William McKinley

24. Who was the first "Baby Boomer" president?

A. Ronald Reagan   C. Gerald Ford

B. Bill Clinton   D. George W. Bush

25. Who became the first unelected president?

A. Theodore Roosevelt   C. Andrew Johnson

B. Harry Truman   D. Gerald Ford

26. Which president was the first to be sworn into office outdoors?

A. *William Henry Harrison*

B. *James Monroe*

C. *George Washington*

D. *Theodore Roosevelt*

27. Which president was the first to use an armored limousine?

A. *Franklin D. Roosevelt*

B. *Harry Truman*

C. *William H. Taft*

D. *John F. Kennedy*

28. Who was the first president to be invited to dine in China's Forbidden City?

A. *Richard Nixon*

B. *Donald Trump*

C. *George H.W. Bush*

D. *Barack Obama*

29. Who was the first president to have electricity in the White House?

A. *Benjamin Harrison*

B. *Theodore Roosevelt*

C. *James Buchanan*

D. *Rutherford B. Hayes*

30. Though a few presidents have married women who had been divorced, who are the only two presidents to have been divorced?

A. *J. Madison, M Van Buren*

B. *H. Truman, W. Harding*

C. *J. Tyler, W. Wilson*

D. *R. Reagan, D. Trump*

Answers

Chapter 7 - I Was The First President To...

1. B - William Henry Harrison

2. C - Franklin D. Roosevelt

He had polio previous to becoming president, though even throughout his presidency many people were unaware he wore braces and couldn't walk without crutches.

3. A - John Adams

He moved in the White House while the paint was still wet in November, 1800.

4. C - Thomas Jefferson

5. C - John Tyler

6. D - Lyndon B. Johnson

7. B - Donald Trump

8. A - Theodore Roosevelt

9. B - Rutherford B. Hayes

Alexander Graham Bell himself installed the telephone. The phone number was #1.

10. B - Ulysses S. Grant

11. D - Woodrow Wilson

12. C - Lyndon B. Johnson

13. A - James Polk

14. C - Barack Obama

15. D - John F. Kennedy

16. D - John Quincy Adams

17. A - Warren Harding

18. B - Martin Van Buren

The previous presidents all were born prior to the Declaration of Independence so were born British subjects.

19. C - Dwight D. Eisenhower

20. C - Donald Trump

While all of the answers given were businessmen before becoming president, Donald Trump is the only one who was not involved in politics (other than donating to politicians campaigns) before becoming president.

21. A - Andrew Johnson

22. B - Barack Obama

23. A - Richard Nixon

24. B - Bill Clinton

25. D - Gerald Ford

26. B - James Monroe

27. A - Franklin D. Roosevelt

The limousine originally belonged to Al Capone, a gangster. The Secret Service needed a car to drive President Roosevelt to deliver his speech on Pearl Harbor the day after they were attacked. The Treasury Department had impounded Capone's armored car years earlier so it was available for the president's use.

28. B – Donald Trump

29. A - Benjamin Harrison

30. D - Ronald Reagan, Donald Trump

8

I Was The One & Only President To...

Answers are given on page 56.

1. Who was the only president to serve two terms not in succession?

   A. Franklin D. Roosevelt   *C. George Washington*

   B. John Adams   *D. Grover Cleveland*

2. Which president due to not trusting the mainstream media was the only president to have used "tweets" to communicate with the public?

   A. George W. Bush   *C. Donald Trump*

   B. Bill Clinton   *D. Barack Obama*

3. Who was the only unanimously elected president by the Electoral College?

   A. Ronald Reagan   *C. John F. Kennedy*

   B. Franklin D. Roosevelt   *D. George Washington*

4. What president became both vice-president and president without being elected to either office?

A. George Washington   C. Gerald Ford

B. Thomas Jefferson   D. George H.W. Bush

5. Which president was the only man to serve both as president and as chief justice?

A. William H. Taft   C. George Washington

B. Grover Cleveland   D. Thomas Jefferson

6. Who was the only president elected to serve more than two terms?

A. Grover Cleveland   C. George Washington

B. Franklin D. Roosevelt   D. Abraham Lincoln

7. Who was the only president that didn't represent a political party?

A. Donald Trump   C. Abraham Lincoln

B. Thomas Jefferson   D. George Washington

8. Who was the only president who had two assassination attempts against him made by women?

A. Ronald Reagan   C. Gerald Ford

B. William McKinley   D. George H.W. Bush

9. Who was the only president to resign?

A. Donald Trump   C. Gerald Ford

B. *Ulysses S. Grant*   D. *Richard Nixon*

10. Who was the only bachelor president in American history?

A. *James Buchanan*   C. *Martin Van Buren*

B. *Thomas Jefferson*   D. *Andrew Jackson*

11. Who was the only president to have been married in the White House?

A. *Woodrow Wilson*   C. *William H. Taft*

B. *Grover Cleveland*   D. *Chester Arthur*

12. Who was the only president to have also have been the director of the CIA?

A. *Franklin D. Roosevelt*   C. *Dwight D. Eisenhower*

B. *George H.W. Bush*   D. *Herbert Hoover*

Answers

Chapter 8 - I Was The One & Only President To...

1. D - Grover Cleveland

2. C - Donald Trump

3. D - George Washington

James Monroe, the fifth president, received every Electoral College vote except for one. A New Hampshire delegate wanted to preserve the legacy of George Washington, and that is the only reason he didn't receive all the Electoral College votes.

4. C - Gerald Ford

5. A - William Howard Taft

He was the only man in history to hold the highest position in not only the executive branch but also the judicial branch of the government

6. B - Franklin Roosevelt

He was the only president to have been elected as president four times. After he served as president, the Twenty-Second Amendment was ratified in 1951 which limited the presidential office to two terms.

7. D - George Washington

8. C - Gerald Ford

9. D - Richard Nixon

10. A - James Buchanan

11. B - Grover Cleveland

12. B – George H.W. Bush

9

Vice President: The Man In The Shadows

Answers are given on page 60 - 62.

1. Which vice president said he invented the internet?

A. Joe Biden

C. Al Gore

B. Dan Quayle

D. Mike Pence

2. Which vice president is best known for shooting and killing Alexander Hamilton in a duel in 1804?

A. John Adams

C. Elbridge Gerry

B. John Calhoun

D. Aaron Burr

3. Who was the vice president while visiting a school told a student that he spelled the word potato wrong that it needed an e on the end? The student was obviously correct and the vice president learned a harsh lesson that the mainstream media would never let him forget. Who was he?

A. Dan Quayle

C. George HW Bush

B. Al Gore   D. Lyndon B Johnson

4. Who is the the only vice president to assume office outside the United States ?

A. Daniel Tompkins   C. William King

B. George Clinton   D. Hannibal Hamlin

5. Who was the first vice president to assume the office of the presidency after the death of a sitting president?

A. John Tyler   C. Andrew Johnson

B. Millard Fillmore   D. Chester Arthur

6. Which former vice president's hidden secret life was revealed when he died while fornicating with his mistress?

A. Lyndon B. Johnson   C. Walter Mondale

B. Nelson Rockefeller   D. Adlai Stephenson

7. Which vice president was involved and exposed in his covert operation supplying the Nicaraguan Contras with arms, cash, and supplies?

A. George H.W. Bush   C. Dick Cheney

B. *Walter Mondale*   D. *Joe Biden*

8. Which of our vice presidents was the only one to ever resign due to scandal?

A. *Aaron Burr*   C. *Spiro Agnew*

B. *Andrew Johnson*   D. *Hubert Humphrey*

9. Which vice president is said to have taken his oath of office drunk?

A. *Chester Arthur*   C. *Mike Pence*

B. *Levi Morton*   D. *Andrew Johnson*

10. Which of our vice presidents accidentally shot his hunting partner shooting him in the face, neck, and chest?

A. *Garret Hobart*   C. *Theodore Roosevelt*

B. *Dick Cheney*   D. *Al Gore*

Answers

Chapter 9 - Vice President: The Man In The Shadows

1. C - Al Gore, vice president to Bill Clinton

2. D – Aaron Burr, vice president to Thomas Jefferson

 * *Not only did he kill Hamilton in a duel, but few people are aware he also plotted a treasonous conspiracy to become emperor of the western United States and Mexico. He was tried for his treasonous conspiracy plot in 1807 before the Supreme Court, which found him not guilty, largely in part because he hadn't actually committed the treason at that point. A free man, Burr still hadn't learned his lesson as he at that point turned his sights on Florida.*

3. A - Dan Quayle, vice president to George H.W. Bush

 * *Dan Quayle is considered to have been one of the most active Vice Presidents in history. Dan Quayle became one of the most admired Americans of his time, but on this day he became a laughingstock and that's what he was most remembered for. You know the saying: Do 1,000 good things, but mess up once and that's what the people remember.*

4. C - William King, vice president to Franklin Pierce

 **William Rufus King, vice president to Franklin Pierce, was sworn into office in 1853 near Havana. He remains to this day the only vice president to have been sworn into office on foreign soil. He had gone to Cuba to recuperate from tuberculosis and alcoholism, but was unsuccessful at both. He was vice president for only 25 days. What he is most remembered for though is that it was rumored that he was* homosexual. *The fact that he flaunted wearing wigs and scarves fanned the flames of the rumor.*

5. A - John Tyler – vice president to William Henry Harrison

* *John Tyler became the first president to rise by succession from the vice presidency after William H. Harrison died of pneumonia a month after being sworn into office.*

6. B - Nelson Rockefeller vice president to Gerald Ford

* *Rockefeller's 27 year old mistress, Megan Marshak, was pinned underneath Rockefeller who was a large man when he collapsed having a heart attack while having sexual intercourse with his mistress. The fact that he was a large man she struggled to get out from under him. The fact that it wasn't known to the public that he had a mistress she decided instead of calling for an ambulance to call a friend who lived close by. After the friend arrived it was a full hour after he had collapsed before her friend finally had the presence of mind to call for an ambulance. When medical help arrived he was still alive and died en route to the hospital. Who knows if he would have survived if medical help would have been called immediately. Happy, Rockefeller's wife, was anything but happy and had his body cremated only hours after he passed away. Nelson Rockefeller had been one of the most powerful and famous men of his time, a multi-millionaire, a grandson of John D. Rockefeller, and a former vice president and governor of New York.*

7. A - George H.W. Bush, vice president to Ronald Reagan

George H.W. Bush was a congressman, ambassador, director of CIA, vice-president & president. Just don't look too close! Lots of skeletons in his closets. No surprise there as he was director of the CIA whose name these days is as dirty as the mud pies you played in as a kid. It has been revealed that it was Vice President Bush and not the CIA (which isn't much of a difference as he had been director of CIA before becoming VP so he definitely knew how to play the game) who was linked to supplying the Nicaraguan Contras with weapons.

8. C - Spiro Agnew, vice president to Richard Nixon

* October of 1973, after months of pressure and scandal, Vice President Spiro Agnew turned in his letter of resignation to President Nixon (who was soon to follow him) becoming the first vice president to resign due to scandal and only the second vice president to resign. (The first vice president to resign was John Calhoun due to political differences with President Andrew Jackson.) Spiro Agnew is the only Vice President in U.S. history to have resigned due to criminal charges. It was his fifth year in office when the U.S. Attorney's office in the state of Maryland began investigating the VP for bribery, tax fraud, extortion and conspiracy. Agnew was charged in October for having accepted more than $100,000 in bribes during his time as Vice President and Governor of Maryland; he was allowed to plead no contest on the condition that he resign.

9. D - Andrew Johnson – vice president to Abraham Lincoln

10. B - Dick Cheney – vice president to George W Bush

10

First Lady: The Woman Behind The Man

Answers are given on page 69 - 70.

1. Which First Lady danced to disco music at informal White House events?

A. Nancy Reagan

B. Barbara Bush

C. Betty Ford

D. Michelle Obama

2. Who was the youngest First Lady in American history?

A. Frances Cleveland

B. Michelle Obama

C. Jackie Kennedy

D. Melania Trump

3. I was wife of one President, grandmother to another President, yet I never set foot in the White House. Who am I?

A. Martha Washington

B. Eliza Johnson

C. Abigail Adams

D. Anna Harrison

4. Some visitors at the presidential mansion called this First Lady, "Our Lady Presidentess." Who was she?

    A. Edith Wilson   C. Dolley Madison

    B. Martha Washington   D. Louisa Adams

5. Which First Lady is fluent in 6 languages?

    A. Louisa Adams   C. Lou Hoover

    B. Jackie Kennedy   D. Melania Trump

6. She was one of the most accomplished First Ladies as a lawyer, First Lady, and after her time in the White House became a senator, presidential candidate, and Secretary of State, but she has also been linked with more scandals than any other First Ladies.

    A. Michelle Obama   C. Hillary Clinton

    B. Lady Bird Johnson   D. Eleanor Roosevelt

7. Which First Lady was an Ivy League graduate?

    A. Hillary Clinton   C. Lady Bird Johnson

    B. Lou Hoover   D. Michelle Obama

8. Which two presidential widows are the only ones to have remarried?

A. F. Cleveland & J. Kennedy

C. F. Cleveland & G. Coolidge

B. L. Adams & L. Garfield

D. L. Hoover & J. Kennedy

9. Which First Lady was not only First Lady; but the wife of a Civil War General?

A. Dolley Madison

C. Margaret "Peggy" Taylor

B. Anna Harrison

D. Julia Grant

10. Described as warm and down-to-earth, she kept her door closed to all interview requests.

A. Melania Trump

C. Laura Bush

B. Bess Truman

D. Lady Bird Johnson

11. I was an actress. Who am I?

A. Betty Ford

C. Melania Trump

B. Jackie Kennedy

D. Nancy Reagan

12. On the Larry King Live show, which First Lady spoke in support of legalizing same-sex marriage and keeping abortion legal?

A. Laura Bush   C. Betty Ford

B. Barbara Bush   D. Pat Nixon

13. She is the First Lady most noted for her love of nature and the importance she put on conserving the environment.

A. Michelle Obama   C. Rosalyn Carter

B. Lady Bird Johnson   D. Eleanor Roosevelt

14. She was the 1st First Lady to travel with the President to the People's Republic of China and to a summit meeting in the Soviet Union.

A. Pat Nixon   C. Laura Bush

B. Julia Grant   D. Barbara Bush

15. We are the only 2 foreign born First Ladies. Who are we?

A. I. McKinley & H. Van Buren   C. L. Adams & M. Trump

B. L. Tyler & M. Trump   D. L. Garfield & M. Trump

16. Who is the only woman to not only be the First Lady, but also the wife of the Chief Justice of the U.S. Supreme Court?

A. Helen Taft   C. Eleanor Roosevelt

B. *Mamie Eisenhower*   D. *Ida McKinley*

17. This First Lady surprised the Chinese when they took her to a commune and she told them how she raised pigs on a farm when she was a young girl.

A. *Laura Bush*   C. *Pat Nixon*

B. *Julia Grant*   D. *Melania Trump*

18. Who was the longest serving First Lady?

A. *Frances Cleveland*   C. *Hillary Clinton*

B. *Martha Washington*   D. *Eleanor Roosevelt*

19. In 2008, she ran unsuccessfully for the Democratic presidential nomination. She ran again in the 2016 presidential race and lost again and is linked with the Uranium One Scandal.

A. *Bess Truman*   C. *Mamie Eisenhower*

B. *Hillary Clinton*   D. *Michelle Obama*

20. She often was criticized for her lavish, extravagant, and extensive travels abroad when the nation was suffering from hard economic times.

A. *Michelle Obama*   C. *Laura Bush*

B. Melania Trump   *D. Jackie Kennedy*

Answers

Chapter 10 – First Lady: The Woman Behind The Man

1. C - Betty Ford, wife of Gerald Ford

2. A - Frances Cleveland, wife of Grover Cleveland

3. D - Anna Harrison, wife of William H. Harrison

4. B - Martha Washington, wife of George Washington

5. D – Melania Trump, wife of Donald Trump

   Melania Trump speaks English, Slovenian, French, Italian, German, and Serbo-Croatian.

6. C - Hillary Clinton, wife of Bill Clinton

7. D - Michelle Obama, wife of Barack Obama

8. A - Frances Cleveland, wife of Grover Cleveland & Jackie Kennedy, wife of John F. Kennedy

9. D - Julia Grant, wife of Ulysses S. Grant

10. B - Bess Truman, wife of Harry Truman

11. D - Nancy Reagan, wife of Ronald Reagan

12. A - Laura Bush, wife of George W. Bush

13. B - Lady Bird Johnson, wife of Lyndon B. Johnson

14. A - Pat Nixon, wife of Richard Nixon

15. C - Louisa Adams, wife of John Quincy Adams & Melania Trump, wife of Donald Trump

16. A - Helen "Nellie" Taft, wife of William H. Taft

17. C - Pat Nixon, wife of Richard Nixon

18. D - Eleanor Roosevelt, wife of Franklin D. Roosevelt

19. B - Hillary Clinton, wife of Bill Clinton

20. A - Michelle Obama, wife of Barack Obama

11

First Family: Children In The White House

Answers are given on page 76 - 77.

1. Which president's son brought hungry children, which the White House kitchen called "street urchins," in to be fed at the White House?

A. Jacky Washington

B. Elliott Roosevelt

C. Allan Hoover

D. Tad Lincoln

2. Which president's son on his first night in the White House went on the roof with his stereo playing Led Zeppelin?

A. Chip Carter

B. Donald Trump Jr

C. Steve Ford

D. Michael Reagan

3. Which president's daughter after staying overnight in the Lincoln Bedroom swore she had seen Lincoln's ghost?

A. Martha Jefferson

B. Maureen Reagan

C. Mollie Garfield

D. Sasha Obama

4. Which president's son had a butler replaced just because he didn't like the way he walked?

A. *Allan Hoover*   C. *Payne Madison*

B. *Smith Van Buren*   D. *Ron Reagan*

5. The first lady gave her daughters the advice, "Don't do anything you wouldn't mind seeing on the front page of the newspaper?" Which president's daughters received this advice?

A. *Jessie & Margaret Wilson*   C. *Malia & Sasha Obama*

B. *Lynda & Luci Johnson*   D. *Julie & Tricia Nixon*

6. Which president's daughter was reclusive to the point that her sister referred to her as, "the Howard Hughes of the White House?"

A. *Caroline Kennedy*   C. *Tricia Nixon*

B. *Amy Carter*   D. *Luci Johnson*

7. Which president's daughter had a pony named Macaroni that she rode on the White House lawn?

A. *Ethel Roosevelt*   C. *Anna Roosevelt*

B. *Eleanor Wilson*   D. *Caroline Kennedy*

8. Which president's daughter milked the cows from the White House dairy every morning?

A. *Nell Arthur*   C. *Ruth Cleveland*

B. *Martha Johnson*   D. *Elizabeth Monroe*

9. Which president's daughter was taught to drive at Camp David in an

armored Secret Service car?

    A. Chelsea Clinton   *C. Tricia Nixon*

    B. Malia Obama   *D. Susan Ford*

10. Which presidential son's most memorable experience while living in the White House was to see a Wright Brother's flying machine land on the South Lawn of the White House?

    A. Charlie Taft   *C. Manning Force Hayes*

    B. Smith Van Buren   *D. Archie Roosevelt*

11. Which president's daughter dated movie star George Hamilton?

    A. Tricia Nixon   *C. Alice Roosevelt*

    B. Margaret Truman   *D. Lynda Johnson*

12. Which president's son carved his initials in the presidential yacht?

    A. Chip Carter   *C. Charlie Taft*

    B. Tad Lincoln   *D. None of the above*

13. Which president's daughter was an only child of a president?

    A. Margaret Truman   *C. Ivanka Trump*

    B. Luci Johnson   *D. Chelsea Clinton*

14. Which presidential daughter was scandalous, doing things such as smoking in public that young women of the times didn't do; yet the

public and the press loved her wondering what scandalous thing she would do next?

A. Knoxie Taylor

C. Nellie Grant

B. Alice Roosevelt

D. Margaret Truman

15. Which president's son tied goats to a chair and had them pull him through the East Room of the White House chariot style?

A. John Kennedy Jr

C. Barron Trump

B. Quentin Roosevelt

D. Tad Lincoln

16. Which president's sons and friends threw spitballs at President Andrew Jackson's portrait?

A. Sons of T. Roosevelt

C. Sons of F. D. Roosevelt

B. Sons of D. Trump

D. Sons of J. Madison

17. Name the only two presidents to have a child born during their administration.

A. T. Jefferson & G. Cleveland

C. W. Harding & B. Clinton

B. Cleveland & J.F Kennedy

D. None of the above

18. Which First Family member, along with the First Lady, was taught to dance the Charleston by the White House butler – even though the President refused to let his family dance in public?

A. John Coolidge

C. Caroline Kennedy

B. Jessie Wilson

D. Herbert Hoover Jr

19. During her father's administration, which president's daughter led marches for women's rights and organized protests and pushed her father into supporting the 19th Amendment giving women the right to vote?

A. Anna Roosevelt   *C. Jessie Wilson*

B. Nell Arthur   *D. Alice Roosevelt*

20. Name one of the presidents sons who enjoyed going to the White House roof to watch the stars through a telescope.

A. Allan Hoover   *C. Jeff Carter*

B. Marvin Bush   *D. Jessie Grant*

Answers

Chapter 11 – First Family: Children In The White House

1. D – Tad Lincoln

2. C – Steve Ford

3. B – Maureen Reagan

4. A – Allan Hoover

5. B – Lynda & Luci Johnson

6. C – Tricia Nixon

7. D – Caroline Kennedy

8. B – Martha Johnson

9. A – Chelsea Clinton

10. A – Charlie Taft

11. D – Lynda Johnson

12. C – Charlie Taft

13. A – Margaret Truman or D – Chelsea Clinton, both were only children

14. B – Alice Roosevelt

15. D – Tad Lincoln

16. A – Sons of Roosevelt

17. B – Grover Cleveland & John F Kennedy

18. A – John Coolidge

19. C – Jessie Wilson

20. Either one is correct: C – Jeff Carter *or*   D – Jessie Grant

12

Remarkable Feats

Answers are given on page 88 - 91.

1. Which president created the interstate highway system?

    A. Franklin D. Roosevelt   *C. Jimmy Carter*

    B. Lyndon B. Johnson   *D. Dwight D. Eisenhower*

2. Which president was responsible for keeping the Union intact?

    A. Dwight D. Eisenhower   *C. James Buchanan*

    B. Abraham Lincoln   *D. Ulysses S. Grant*

3. Which president signed the treaty to purchase Alaska from Russia?

    A. Andrew Johnson   *C. James Buchanan*

    B. Chester Arthur   *D. Theodore Roosevelt*

4. Which president officially ended the U.S. involvement in the Vietnam War?

    A. Lyndon B. Johnson   *C. Richard Nixon*

    B. Gerald Ford   *D. Jimmy Carter*

5. Which president's greatest achievement is considered to be The Affordable Care Act?

   A. Lyndon B. Johnson   *C. Barack Obama*

   B. Jimmy Carter   *D. Herbert Hoover*

6. Which president expanded the American boundaries to the Pacific Ocean?

   A. James Polk   *C. Rutherford B. Hayes*

   B. William McKinley   *D. Thomas Jefferson*

7. Which president recognized the state of Israel when it declared itself a nation?

   A. George H.W. Bush   *C. Harry Truman*

   B. Barack Obama   *D. Richard Nixon*

8. Which president brought home the P.O.W.'s from Vietnam?

   A. Lyndon B. Johnson   *C. Jimmy Carter*

   B. Richard Nixon   *D. Ronald Reagan*

9. Which president issued the Emancipation Proclamation?

   A. Abraham Lincoln   *C. Donald Trump*

   B. Thomas Jefferson   *D. John F. Kennedy*

10. Which president created the departments: Department of Energy and

the Department of Education?

A. Harry Truman   C. Jimmy Carter

B. John F. Kennedy   D. Lyndon B. Johnson

11. Which president was responsible for deactivating more than 1,700 nuclear warheads from the former Soviet Union?

A. Ronald Reagan   C. George H.W. Bush

B. Bill Clinton   D. Dwight D. Eisenhower

12. Who was president when America's territory grew by more than one-third extending out west, which caused a major fight between the northern and southern states over slavery?

A. James Buchanan   C. James Polk

B. Andrew Johnson   D. Abraham Lincoln

13. Which president signed the Indian Citizenship Act? This granted citizenship to Native Americans and allowed them to retain tribal land rights.

A. Calvin Coolidge   C. Andrew Jackson

B. Warren Harding   D. Theodore Roosevelt

14. Which president helped reduce tensions with the Soviet Union when he signed the Helsinki Accords?

A. Ronald Reagan   C. John F. Kennedy

B. George H.W. Bush   D. Gerald Ford

15. Which president presided over meetings at Camp David with Egypt's president and Israel's prime minister? The result of these meetings ended the state of war between the two nations for which this president was awarded the Nobel Peace Prize.

A. Barack Obama

C. Jimmy Carter

B. John F. Kennedy

D. Donald Trump

16. Which president founded the Environmental Protection Agency?

A. Theodore Roosevelt

C. George W. Bush

B. Richard Nixon

D. Barack Obama

17. Which president signed the Civil Rights Act that extended the rights of emancipated slaves?

A. Ulysses S. Grant

C. Abraham Lincoln

B. Andrew Johnson

D. Benjamin Harrison

18. Which president visited both China and the Soviet Union to reduce tensions between these countries and the United States?

A. Richard Nixon

C. Ulysses S. Grant

B. George H.W. Bush

D. Jimmy Carter

19. Which president established Social Security?

A. Thomas Jefferson

C. Herbert Hoover

B. William H. Taft

D. Franklin D. Roosevelt

20. Which president signed the Civil Rights Acts of 1964 and 1968?

A. John F. Kennedy   C. Lyndon B. Johnson

B. Jimmy Carter   D. Richard Nixon

21. Which president, on his third day in office, signed an executive action withdrawing the U.S. from the Trans-Pacific Partnership?

A. John F. Kennedy   C. Woodrow Wilson

B. Donald Trump   D. Dwight D. Eisenhower

22. Which president established the Family and Medical Leave Act?

A. Barack Obama   C. John F. Kennedy

B. George W. Bush   D. Bill Clinton

23. Which president negotiated the Nuclear Test – Ban treaty?

A. John F. Kennedy   C. Ronald Reagan

B. Harry Truman   D. Dwight D. Eisenhower

24. Which president led the U.S. from isolationism to a victory over Nazi Germany and their allies during WWII?

A. William H. Taft   C. Woodrow Wilson

B. Franklin D. Roosevelt   D. Herbert Hoover

25. Which president had some of his greatest achievements in the area of conservation?

A. Gerald Ford   C. Theodore Roosevelt

B. John Tyler   D. Bill Clinton

26. Which president created programs to tackle poverty such as: Head Start, food stamps, Medicare, and Medicaid?

A. Lyndon B. Johnson   C. Harry Truman

B. Franklin D. Roosevelt   D. Herbert Hoover

27. Which president signed the Nineteenth Amendment granting women the right to vote?

A. James Garfield   C. Benjamin Harrison

B. William H. Taft   D. Woodrow Wilson

28. Which president ended the draft?

A. Richard Nixon   C. Lyndon B. Johnson

B. Dwight D. Eisenhower   D. Jimmy Carter

29. Which president signed peace treaties with Germany and Austria after WWI?

A. Woodrow Wilson   C. Warren Harding

B. William McKinley   D. Calvin Coolidge

30. Which president significantly lowered tax rates for nearly all U.S. tax payers?

A. Barack Obama   C. Donald Trump

B. George W. Bush   D. Ronald Reagan

31. Which president was responsible for nuclear weapons cuts?

A. Ronald Reagan   C. John F. Kennedy

B. Harry Truman   D. Dwight D. Eisenhower

32. Which president established the Department of Homeland Security?

A. Barack Obama   C. Ronald Reagan

B. George W. Bush   D. Bill Clinton

33. Which president signed The Missouri Compromise?

A. Thomas Jefferson   C. James Madison

B. John Quincy Adams   D. James Monroe

34. Which president signed the Paris Peace Accords ending U.S. involvement in the Vietnam War?

A. Lyndon B. Johnson   C. Richard Nixon

B. John F. Kennedy   D. Gerald Ford

35. Which president issued the doctrine that would contain communism?

A. Ronald Reagan   C. Dwight D. Eisenhower

B. Harry Truman   D. George W. Bush

36. As a conservationist, which president preserved approximately two hundred million acres for wildlife refugees, national forests, and reserves – which was five times the amount of land all his predecessors combined preserved?

A. Andrew Jackson

B. Chester Arthur

C. Grover Cleveland

D. Theodore Roosevelt

37. Which president fulfilled every single one of his campaign promises while serving only one term of office?

A. John Adams

B. John Quincy Adams

C. James Polk

D. James Buchanan

38. Which president kept America at peace, even though he was faced with major Cold War issues every year he was in office?

A. Dwight D. Eisenhower

B. Ronald Reagan

C. George H.W. Bush

D. Bill Clinton

39. Which president prevented nuclear Armageddon?

A. Barack Obama

B. John F. Kennedy

C. Jimmy Carter

D. Harry Truman

40. Which president was responsible for the Monroe Doctrine?

A. James Monroe

B. Thomas Jefferson

C. John Quincy Adams

D. James Madison

41. Who was president when the new treaty the Gadsden Purchase *(land the U.S. purchased via a treaty that consists of present-day southern Arizona and southwestern New Mexico)* was signed?

   A. William McKinley   *C. Franklin Pierce*

   B. James Polk   *D. James Buchanan*

42. Which president drastically reduced unemployment from 25% - 2%?

   A. Bill Clinton   *C. Donald Trump*

   B. John F. Kennedy   *D. Franklin D. Roosevelt*

43. Which president used atomic bombs on Hiroshima and Nagasaki forcing Japan to surrender and ending the war?

   A. Dwight D. Eisenhower   *C. Franklin D. Roosevelt*

   B. Harry Truman   *D. Calvin Coolidge*

44. Who was president when the Louisiana Purchase came about?

   A. James Madison   *C. Thomas Jefferson*

   B. James Monroe   *D. John Quincy Adams*

45. Which president balanced the budget – not just once; but three times?

   A. Dwight D. Eisenhower   *C. Bill Clinton*

   B. Jimmy Carter   *D. Barack Obama*

46. Which president promoted public works such as the Hoover Dam?

A. *Franklin D. Roosevelt*   C. *Calvin Coolidge*

B. *Herbert Hoover*   D. *Theodore Roosevelt*

47. With the Oregon Treaty of 1846, this president acquired a substantial amount of land for the U.S. from the British without having to go to war to do so. Who was he?

A. *James Polk*   C. *William H. Harrison*

B. *Millard Fillmore*   D. *James Buchanan*

48. Which president established the Peace Corps?

A. *Lyndon B. Johnson*   C. *George W. Bush*

B. *Jimmy Carter*   D. *John F. Kennedy*

49. Who was president when the Treaty of Ghent was signed by British and American representatives ending the War of 1812?

A. *Thomas Jefferson*   C. *James Madison*

B. *John Quincy Adams*   D. *Martin Van Buren*

50. Which president oversaw desegregation peacefully of the schools in the South?

A. *Lyndon B. Johnson*   C. *Jimmy Carter*

B. *Richard Nixon*   D. *John F. Kennedy*

Answers

Chapter 12 – Remarkable Feats

1. D - Dwight D. Eisenhower

2. B - Abraham Lincoln

3. A - Andrew Johnson

It is considered his most important foreign policy action.

4. B - Gerald Ford

5. C - Barack Obama

Obamacare or The Affordable Care Act while considered Obama's greatest achievement many will argue that fact considering it was promised that people who were presently uninsured would now be insured; this was not found to be true as the poor still couldn't afford the premiums and still found themselves uninsured, deductibles and premiums soared, the promise of being able to keep your own insurance or doctor were not true, increased America's debt problems, and became a deterrent to new doctors entering the field. The Affordable Care Act appeared to have brought on more problems than it solved – so was this an achievement or a failure?

6. A - James Polk

7. C - Harry Truman

8. B - Richard Nixon

9. A - Abraham Lincoln

10. C - Jimmy Carter

11. B - Bill Clinton

12. C - James Polk

13. A - Calvin Coolidge

14. D - Gerald Ford

15. C - Jimmy Carter

16. B - Richard Nixon

17. A - Ulysses S. Grant

18. A - Richard Nixon

19. D - Franklin D. Roosevelt

20. C - Lyndon B. Johnson

21. B - Donald Trump

22. D - Bill Clinton

23. A - John F. Kennedy

24. B - Franklin D. Roosevelt

25. C - Theodore Roosevelt

26. A - Lyndon B. Johnson

27. D - Woodrow Wilson

28. A - Richard Nixon

29. C - Warren Harding

30. B - George W. Bush

31. A - Ronald Reagan

32. B - George W. Bush

33. D - James Monroe

34. C - Richard Nixon

35. B - Harry Truman

36. D - Theodore Roosevelt

37. C - James Polk

He acquired California from Mexico, settled the Oregon dispute, lowered tariffs, established a sub-treasury, and accomplished it all in one term and then retired from office.

38. A - Dwight D. Eisenhower

39. B - John F. Kennedy

40. A - James Monroe

If you thought this was just too easy so it must be a trick question it was not. If you guessed C – John Quincy Adams, go ahead and give yourself credit as it was J.Q. Adams who not only worded the declaration which became a cornerstone of American foreign policy, but Adams also helped shape the doctrine.

41. C - Franklin Pierce

42. D - Franklin D. Roosevelt

43. B - Harry Truman

While some may argue that this was an achievement, it was a decision that was not easily made, and was successful in bringing an end to the war.

44. C - Thomas Jefferson

45. A - Dwight D. Eisenhower

46. B - Herbert Hoover

47. A - James Polk

This added full control of what is the current states of Washington, Oregon, Idaho, and a portion of what is now the states of Montana and Wyoming.

48. D - John F. Kennedy

49. C- James Madison

The Peace Treaty of Ghent ended the War of 1812.

50. B - Richard Nixon

13

Failures & Embarrassing Moments of the Presidents

Answers are given on page 104 - 106.

1. Which president's biggest failure during his first days as president was his failure to repeal and replace The Affordable Care Act in his first 100 days as promised during his campaign?

A. Barack Obama

C. George W. Bush

B. Donald Trump

D. Bill Clinton

2. Who was president during the Bay of Pigs Invasion?

A. Barack Obama

C. George H.W. Bush

B. Dwight D. Eisenhower

D. John F. Kennedy

3. Who was president when the number of people having to turn to food stamps was at a record high?

A. Herbert Hoover

C. Jimmy Carter

B. Franklin D. Roosevelt

D. Barack Obama

4. Which president failed to defuse the Cold War?

A. *Dwight D. Eisenhower*   C. *Ronald Reagan*

B. *Bill Clinton*   D. *George H.W. Bush*

5. Which president's policy of communist containment is what started the Cold War?

A. *Franklin D. Roosevelt*   C. *Harry Truman*

B. *Herbert Hoover*   D. *John F. Kennedy*

6. Which president fought for gun control, but his legislation requiring background checks on all guns purchased and a ban on assault weapons wasn't approved through Congress?

A. *Bill Clinton*   C. *Donald Trump*

B. *Barack Obama*   D. *Jimmy Carter*

7. Who was president during the "space race" with the Russians which cost American taxpayers $50 billion?

A. *John F. Kennedy*   C. *Ronald Reagan*

B. *Richard Nixon*   D. *George H.W. Bush*

8. Which president failed to heal the nation after the Civil War?

A. *Abraham Lincoln*   C. *Ulysses S. Grant*

B. *James Buchanan*   D. *Andrew Johnson*

9. The Depression worsened during which president's administration?

A. *Franklin D. Roosevelt*   C. *Harry Truman*

B. *Herbert Hoover*   D. *Barack Obama*

10. Which president's medical reform was to ensure *"everyone"* was insured; but not only did that not happen, but this insurance plan came at too high an expense for taxpayers?

A. *Donald Trump*   C. *Franklin D. Roosevelt*

B. *Lyndon B. Johnson*   D. *Barack Obama*

11. The White House knew about the plans for Rwandan genocide and did nothing to stop it. Who was president at the time?

A. *Barack Obama*   C. *Bill Clinton*

B. *George H.W. Bush*   D. *Jimmy Carter*

12. Which president vetoed every equal rights bill that would help African-Americans?

A. *Andrew Johnson*   C. *Ulysses S. Grant*

B. *Warren Harding*   D. *Donald Trump*

13. This president justified the War of Iraq by claiming they had weapons of mass destruction. Who was he?

A. *George H.W. Bush*   C. *Bill Clinton*

B. *Barack Obama*   D. *George W. Bush*

14. Racial divisions worsened during his presidency, instead of healing

like people expected. Who was he?

    A. Franklin D. Roosevelt   *C. Barack Obama*

    B. Lyndon B. Johnson   *D. Donald Trump*

15. Which president helped establish the League of Nations and then failed to join the U.S. as a part?

    A. Woodrow Wilson   *C. Franklin D. Roosevelt*

    B. John F. Kennedy   *D. Harry Truman*

16. Which president fired over one thousand postmasters in the South who weren't sympathetic to his policies? He fired so many that the Tenure of Office Act was passed prohibiting the president from firing any confirmed appointees without having the Senate's approval.

    A. Abraham Lincoln   *C. Andrew Johnson*

    B. Jimmy Carter   *D. Zachary Taylor*

17. Which president failed to free the American hostages in Iran? A failed rescue attempt led his reputation to be inept and ineffective. Who was he?

    A. Lyndon B. Johnson   *C. George H.W. Bush*

    B. Jimmy Carter   *D. Richard Nixon*

18. Who was president when Prohibition, the banning of manufacture, sale, and transporting of alcohol went into effect? This president vetoed the National Prohibition Act, but his veto was overridden by Congress.

    A. Rutherford B. Hayes   *C. William H. Taft*

B. *Woodrow Wilson*   D. *Grover Cleveland*

19. Sex scandals, including but not limited to the actress Marilyn Monroe, left this president with a bad reputation as a womanizer? Who was he?

A. *Bill Clinton*   C. *Warren Harding*

B. *Richard Nixon*   D. *John F. Kennedy*

20. Which president ended the Persian Gulf War without deposing Iraq's dictator, Saddam Hussein?

A. *George H.W. Bush*   C. *Jimmy Carter*

B. *Bill Clinton*   D. *George W. Bush*

21. Who was president when the War of 1812 occurred? Some considered this war a second war for independence, however the United States suffered many costly defeats including the capture and burning of the nation's capital which included the Executive Mansion or White House.

A. *Thomas Jefferson*   C. *James Madison*

B. *John Quincy Adams*   D. *James Monroe*

22. Who was president when the housing market crashed, and it was the beginning of the recession?

A. *George W. Bush*   C. *Herbert Hoover*

B. *Barack Obama*   D. *Theodore Roosevelt*

23. Which president's stimulus did little to stimulate the economy?

A. John F. Kennedy

C. Barack Obama

B. Franklin D. Roosevelt

D. Grover Cleveland

24. Who was president during the rise of McCarthyism?

A. John F. Kennedy

C. Calvin Coolidge

B. Harry Truman

D. Dwight D. Eisenhower

25. Which president failed to turn over documents subpoenaed by Congressional committees and claimed immunity from civil lawsuits claiming presidential immunity?

A. Bill Clinton

C. Richard Nixon

B. Barack Obama

D. Donald Trump

26. Which president was responsible for the passing of the Sherman Silver Purchase Act which depleted the gold supply?

A. Grover Cleveland

C. Andrew Johnson

B. William H. Taft

D. Benjamin Harrison

27. Who was president during the hostage crisis in Iran?

A. Ronald Reagan

C. Jimmy Carter

B. George W. Bush

D. Gerald Ford

28. Which president's 'War On Poverty' had no clear plan on how to go

about fixing the problem and was more talk than action?

A. Andrew Jackson

C. Herbert Hoover

B. James Buchanan

D. Lyndon B. Johnson

29. Who was president during "The Plame Leak" which identified a covert operative in the CIA?

A. George W. Bush

C. Barack Obama

B. George H.W. Bush

D. Bill Clinton

30. In June of 1950, the Korean War began when soldiers from the North Korean People's Army crossed the 38th parallel, the boundary between Soviet backed Democratic People's Republic of Korea to the north and pro-Western Republic of Korea to the south. This invasion was the first military action of the Cold War. America came to the defense of South Korea considering this a war against communism. What president ordered our troops into action to join in to aid South Korea as a "police action"? The fighting ended in July of 1953 when an armistice was signed, however no peace treaty was ever signed and the two Koreas are, *technically* at least, still at war.

A. Dwight D. Eisenhower

C. Harry Truman

B. Calvin Coolidge

D. Franklin D. Roosevelt

31. Which president, and his administration, was involved with the cover up of their involvement of the scandal of Watergate?

A. Bill Clinton

C. Gerald Ford

B. Richard Nixon

D. George H.W. Bush

32. Who was president when the 'The Brownsville Incident' occurred, whose action to the incident has remained a matter of controversy and an embarrassment to the army?

A. Theodore Roosevelt

C. Barack Obama

B. George W. Bush

D. Grover Cleveland

33. Which president is associated with 'The Monica Lewinsky Scandal'?

A. John F. Kennedy

C. James Buchanan

B. Lyndon B. Johnson

D. Bill Clinton

34. Which president relocated Japanese-Americans into internment camps?

A. Abraham Lincoln

C. Franklin D. Roosevelt

B. Zachary Taylor

D. Dwight D. Eisenhower

35. The 'Teapot Dome Scandal' occurred during which president's administration?

A. Franklin D. Roosevelt

C. William H. Taft

B. Warren Harding

D. Grover Cleveland

36. Which president failed to defuse the Cold War and it became even more of a threat at the time he left the presidency than when he began it eight years earlier?

A. Dwight D. Eisenhower

C. John F. Kennedy

B. Jimmy Carter

D. George H.W. Bush

37. Which president gave up on his fight against slavery, deciding to fight only battles he could win?

A. James Buchanan   C. Andrew Johnson

B. Ulysses S. Grant   D. Thomas Jefferson

38. What president was left as a lame duck his final two years in office due to failures in his administration?

A. Barack Obama   C. Donald Trump

B. George W. Bush   D. Jimmy Carter

39. What president's economic decisions were a contributing factor to the Panic of 1837?

A. Andrew Jackson   C. Martin Van Buren

B. Grover Cleveland   D. Millard Fillmore

40. Which president's administration failed at one of it's main objectives which was energy? This president believed it imperative that the U.S. not rely on foreign oil. The result with his fight against foreign oil was long lines at the gas stations and driving up oil prices. Who was he?

A. Lyndon B. Johnson   C. Jimmy Carter

B. George H.W. Bush   D. Barack Obama

41. Which president received illegal campaign contributions by Indonesians which was called 'Indogate', which gave the impression American foreign policy was up for sale?

A. Barack Obama   C. Donald Trump

B. Bill Clinton   D. George W. Bush

42. Who was president during the Iran-Contra Affair?

A. John F. Kennedy   C. George H.W. Bush

B. Dwight D. Eisenhower   D. Ronald Reagan

43. Inconsistent on social issues, what president opposed discrimination against Chinese immigrants, but failed to support women's' right to vote, equality for African-American voting rights, or the rights of American Indians to preserve their culture?

A. Grover Cleveland   C. Franklin D. Roosevelt

B. Andrew Johnson   D. Harry Truman

44. What president promised to ask Great Britain to give Ireland their independence, but failed to do so?

A. John F. Kennedy   C. Woodrow Wilson

B. William McKinley   D. Calvin Coolidge

45. Which president turned Lincoln's historic bedroom into a means of receiving large donations or basically rented out Lincoln's room for the right price?

A. Bill Clinton   C. Barack Obama

B. Donald Trump   D. John F. Kennedy

46. Which president brought in his daughter and son-in-law as senior

advisors to work with him in the White House which the American public considered nepotism?

A. Andrew Johnson

B. Franklin D. Roosevelt

C. Rutherford B. Hayes

D. Donald Trump

47. Which president's Embargo Act, which restricted trade, ended up hurting Americans more than Britain or France who it was originally intended to hurt?

A. John Adams

B. Thomas Jefferson

C. John Quincy Adams

D. James Madison

48. Which president failed to deal with the issue of slavery, instead leaving the matter for the states and territories to decide for themselves?

A. James Buchanan

B. Ulysses S. Grant

C. Abraham Lincoln

D. James Garfield

49. The Depression didn't end until the start of WWII. Who was president during the time of the Great Depression?

A. Theodore Roosevelt

B. George W. Bush

C. Franklin D. Roosevelt

D. Warren Harding

50. Which president tied up four runways at Los Angeles International Airport, one of the busiest airports in the nation, for nearly an hour while Air Force One's engines were running, just so the president could get his hair trimmed?

A. John F. Kennedy

C. Barack Obama

B. Donald Trump   *D. Bill Clinton*

B. Donald Trump   *D. Bill Clinton*

Answers

Chapter 13 – Failures & Embarrassing Moments of the Presidents

1. B - Donald Trump

2. D - John F. Kennedy

3. D - Barack Obama

4. A - Dwight D. Eisenhower

5. C - Harry Truman

6. B - Barack Obama

7. A - John F. Kennedy

8. D - Andrew Johnson

9. B - Herbert Hoover

10. D -Barack Obama

11. C - Bill Clinton

12. A - Andrew Johnson

13. D - George W. Bush

14. C - Barack Obama

15. A - Woodrow Wilson

16. C - Andrew Johnson

17. B - Jimmy Carter

18. B - Woodrow Wilson

19. D - John F. Kennedy

20. A - George H.W. Bush

21. C - James Madison

22. A - George W. Bush

23. C - Barack Obama

24. B - Harry Truman

25. A - Bill Clinton

26. D - Benjamin Harrison

27. C - Jimmy Carter

28. D - Lyndon B. Johnson

29. A - George W. Bush

30. C - Harry Truman

31. B - Richard Nixon

32. A - Theodore Roosevelt

33. D - Bill Clinton

34. C - Franklin D. Roosevelt

35. B - Warren Harding

36. A - Dwight D. Eisenhower

37. D - Thomas Jefferson

38. B - George W. Bush

39. A - Andrew Jackson

40. C - Jimmy Carter

41. B - Bill Clinton

42. D - Ronald Reagan

43. A - Grover Cleveland

44. C - Woodrow Wilson

45. A - Bill Clinton

46. D - Donald Trump

Not only does this scream of nepotism but is also unethical. While in the early days of the presidents many presidential sons worked closely by their father's sides in the White House and received esteemed appointments, but such signs of nepotism hasn't been seen in the White House since the days of John F. Kennedy when he hired his own brother as attorney general and his brother-in-law Sargent Shriver also served in his administration. In 1967 the Federal Anti-Nepotism Statute, known as Section 3110, was passed.

President Trump gets around this by stating that they are "unpaid" advisors. While it is true that it has been proven that the president can't trust many of those even on his own staff and most likely feels he can trust his own family members, many consider Ivanka and Jared Kushner to have their own agendas and the American public didn't vote for a Trump dynasty.

47. B -Thomas Jefferson

48. A - James Buchanan

49. C - Franklin D. Roosevelt

50. D – Bill Clinton

14

Words of Wisdom

Answers are given on page 118 - 120.

1. "It is not strange...to mistake change for progress."

    A. Millard Fillmore   *C. Barack Obama*

    B. Theodore Roosevelt   *D. Donald Trump*

2. "Change will not come if we wait for some other person, or if we wait for some other time. We are the ones we've been waiting for. We are the change that we seek."

    A. Abraham Lincoln   *C. Ronald Reagan*

    B. George W. Bush   *D. Barack Obama*

3. "If you want to make enemies, try to change something."

    A. Woodrow Wilson   *C. Calvin Coolidge*

    B. Donald Trump   *D. Jimmy Carter*

4. "I have never been hurt by what I have not said."

    A. Dwight D. Eisenhower   *C. Richard Nixon*

B. Calvin Coolidge   D. Ronald Reagan

5. "This is more work than in my previous life."

    A. Ulysses S. Grant   C. Donald Trump

    B. George W. Bush   D. Warren Harding

6. "A little rebellion now and then is a good thing, as necessary in the political world as storms in the physical."

    A. Thomas Jefferson   C. Zachary Taylor

    B. Warren Harding   D. John Adams

7. "In this present crisis, government is not the solution to our problems; government is the problem."

    A. John Adams   C. William Henry Harrison

    B. Gerald Ford   D. Ronald Reagan

8. "We Americans have no commission from God to police the world."

    A. Benjamin Harrison   C. George H.W. Bush

    B. Woodrow Wilson   D. Donald Trump

9. "That's the good thing about being president, I can do whatever I want."

    A. George W. Bush   C. Calvin Coolidge

    B. Barack Obama   D. Donald Trump

10. "It takes a great man to be a good listener."

A. Ronald Reagan   *C. Abraham Lincoln*

B. Calvin Coolidge   *D. Herbert Hoover*

11. "Speak softly, and carry a big stick."

A. Theodore Roosevelt   *C. Lyndon B. Johnson*

B. Herbert Hoover   *D. William McKinley*

12. "The less government interferes with private pursuits, the better for general prosperity."

A. Andrew Johnson   *C. Martin Van Buren*

B. George W. Bush   *D. Theodore Roosevelt*

13. "America will never be destroyed from the outside. If we falter and lose our freedoms, it will be because we destroyed ourselves."

A. George H.W. Bush   *C. Donald Trump*

B. Abraham Lincoln   *D. Franklin D. Roosevelt*

14. "Freedom is never more than one generation away from extinction. We didn't pass it to our children in the blood stream. It must be fought for, protected, and handed on for them to do the same."

A. John Adams   *C. Ronald Reagan*

B. Thomas Jefferson   *D. John F. Kennedy*

15. "If Tyranny and Oppression came to this land, it will be in the guise of fighting a foreign enemy."

    A. James Madison   *C. George H.W. Bush*

    B. John Quincy Adams   *D. Franklin D. Roosevelt*

16. "It is far better to be alone, than to be in bad company."

    A. Ronald Reagan   *C. Donald Trump*

    B. James Garfield   *D. George Washington*

17. "Those who deny freedom to others, deserve it not for themselves."

    A. Donald Trump   *C. Ronald Reagan*

    B. Abraham Lincoln   *D. John F. Kennedy*

18. "Government's first duty is to protect the people, not run their lives."

    A. George W. Bush   *C. Ronald Reagan*

    B. Dwight D. Eisenhower   *D. Thomas Jefferson*

19. "When even one American who has done nothing wrong - is forced by fear to shut his mind and close his mouth – then all Americans are in peril."

    A. Thomas Jefferson   *C. Theodore Roosevelt*

    B. Harry Truman   *D. Donald Trump*

20. "And so my fellow Americans, ask not what your country can do for

you; ask what you can do for your country."

A. John F. Kennedy   C. Barack Obama

B. Ronald Reagan   D. Franklin D. Roosevelt

21. "Politics makes me sick."

A. William Taft   C. Donald Trump

B. Jimmy Carter   D. Ulysses S. Grant

22. "Our Constitution was made only for a moral and religious people. It is wholly inadequate to the government of any other."

A. James Monroe   C. John Adams

B. Millard Fillmore   D. Harry Truman

23. "Prosperity cannot be restored by raids upon the Public Treasury."

A. Herbert Hoover   C. Donald Trump

B. James Monroe   D. Barack Obama

24. "Those who want the government to regulate matters of the mind and spirit are like men who are so afraid of being murdered that they commit suicide to avoid assassination."

A. James Madison   C. William H. Taft

B. Harry Truman   D. Herbert Hoover

25. "Every immigrant who comes here should be required within five

years to learn English or leave the country."

A. Calvin Coolidge   C. Donald Trump

B. Theodore Roosevelt   D. Franklin D. Roosevelt

26. "Let your heart feel for the afflictions and distress of everyone, and let your hand give in proportion to your purse."

A. Ronald Reagan   C. George Washington

B. Herbert Hoover   D. Franklin Pierce

27. "I am proud to be the first American president to come to Kenya – and of course; I'm the first Kenyan-American to be president of the United States."

A. James Monroe   C. Warren Harding

B. Andrew Jackson   D. Barack Obama

28. "No tendency is quite so strong in human nature as the desire to lay down rules of conduct for other people."

A. William Taft   C. Donald Trump

B. Calvin Coolidge   D. Barack Obama

29. "That government is best which governs the least, because it's people discipline themselves."

A. Donald Trump   C. Thomas Jefferson

B. Ronald Reagan   D. Theodore Roosevelt

30. "Blessed are the young; for they shall inherit the national debt."

   A. Herbert Hoover   C. Barack Obama

   B. George W. Bush   D. Richard Nixon

31. "Four score and seven years ago our fathers brought forth on this continent a new nation, conceived in Liberty, and dedicated to the proposition that all men are created equal."

   A. John F. Kennedy   C. Barack Obama

   B. James Buchanan   D. Abraham Lincoln

32. "A government big enough to give you everything you want, is a government big enough to take from you everything you have."

   A. Barack Obama   C. John F. Kennedy

   B. Gerald Ford   D. Lyndon B. Johnson

33. "Honest conviction is my courage, the Constitution is my guide."

   A. Andrew Johnson   C. James Monroe

   B. Ronald Reagan   D. Richard Nixon

34. "Office holders are the agents of the people, not their masters."

   A. Grover Cleveland   C. Jimmy Carter

   B. Woodrow Wilson   D. James Garfield

35. During his campaign for president he repeatedly told voters: "I'll

never tell a lie."

A. George H.W. Bush

C. Jimmy Carter

B. Barack Obama

D. Richard Nixon

36. "I pray Heaven to bestow the best of blessing on this house," (referring to the White House) "and on all that shall hereafter inhabit it. May none but honest and wise men ever rule under this roof."

A. James Monroe

C. Abraham Lincoln

B. John Adams

D. James Buchanan

37. "Read my lips: No new taxes."

A. Bill Clinton

C. George H.W. Bush

B. Jimmy Carter

D. Barack Obama

38. "Within the covers of the Bible are the answers for all the problems men face."

A. Ronald Reagan

C. George Washington

B. James Polk

D. Jimmy Carter

39. "Don't join the book burners. Do not think you are going to conceal thoughts by concealing evidence that they ever existed."

A. John F. Kennedy

C. Dwight D. Eisenhower

B. George H.W. Bush

D. Herbert Hoover

40. "May God save the country, for it is evident that the people will not."

A. John Adams   C. Harry Truman

B. James Buchanan   D. Millard Fillmore

41. "The Constitution preserves the advantage of being armed which Americans possess over the people of almost every other nation, where the governments are afraid to trust the people with arms."

A. James Madison   C. Bill Clinton

B. Dwight D. Eisenhower   D. John F. Kennedy

42. "The most terrifying words in the English language are: 'I'm from the government, and I'm here to help.'"

A. Donald Trump   C. Woodrow Wilson

B. Ronald Reagan   D. Andrew Johnson

43. "We have a tendency to condemn people who are different from us, to define their sins as paramount and our own sinfulness as being insignificant."

A. Bill Clinton   C. Barack Obama

B. Donald Trump   D. Jimmy Carter

44. "It is easier to do a job right, than to explain why you didn't."

A. Dwight D. Eisenhower   C. Harry Truman

B. Martin Van Buren   D. James Madison

45. "Enthusiasm for a cause warps judgment."

    A. Harry Truman   *C. William H. Taft*

    B. Ulysses S. Grant   *D. Franklin Pierce*

46. "Posterity! You will never know how much it cost the present generation to preserve your freedom! I hope you will make a good use of it."

    A. George Washington   *C. Thomas Jefferson*

    B. John Adams   *D. John Tyler*

47. "The truth is that all men having power ought to be mistrusted."

    A. James Madison   *C. Martin Van Buren*

    B. John Quincy Adams   *D. Abraham Lincoln*

48. "Don't pray when it rains, if you don't pray when the sun shines."

    A. Martin Van Buren   *C. Richard Nixon*

    B. Rutherford B. Hayes   *D. Warren Harding*

49. "A president's hardest task is not to do what is right, but to know what is right."

    A. Abraham Lincoln   *C. George Washington*

    B. Woodrow Wilson   *D. Lyndon B. Johnson*

50. "We can have no 50-50 allegiance in this country. Either a man is an

American and nothing else, or he is not an American at all."

A. Franklin D. Roosevelt

C. Donald Trump

B. Theodore Roosevelt

D. Dwight D. Eisenhower

Answers

Chapter 14 – Words Of Wisdom

1. A - Millard Fillmore

2. D - Barack Obama

3. A - Woodrow Wilson

4. B - Calvin Coolidge

5. C - Donald Trump

6. A - Thomas Jefferson

Thomas Jefferson wrote this quote in a letter on January 30, 1787, to James Madison after Shay's Rebellion. Jefferson felt that the people had a right to express their grievances against the government, even if those grievances might take the form of violent action.

7. D - Ronald Reagan

8. A - Benjamin Harrison

9. B - Barack Obama

10. B - Calvin Coolidge

11. A - Theodore Roosevelt

12. C - Martin Van Buren

13. B - Abraham Lincoln

14. C - Ronald Reagan

15. A - James Madison

16. D - George Washington

17. B - Abraham Lincoln

18. C - Ronald Reagan

19. B - Harry Truman

20. A - John F. Kennedy

21. A - William Taft

22. C - John Adams

23. A - Herbert Hoover

24. B - Harry Truman

25. B - Theodore Roosevelt

26. C - George Washington

27. D - Barack Obama

28. A - William Taft

29. C - Thomas Jefferson

30. A - Herbert Hoover

31. A - Andrew Johnson

32. B - Gerald Ford

33. D - George W. Bush

34. A - Grover Cleveland

35. C - Jimmy Carter

36. B - John Adams

37. C - George H.W. Bush

38. A - Ronald Reagan

39. C - Dwight D. Eisenhower

40. D - Millard Fillmore

41. A - James Madison

42. B - Ronald Reagan

43. D - Jimmy Carter

44. B - Martin Van Buren

45. C - William H. Taft

46. B - John Adams

47. A - James Madison

48. C - Richard Nixon

49. D - Lyndon B. Johnson

50. B - Theodore Roosevelt

15

War Hawks & War Doves

Answers are given on page 132 - 134.

1. How many future presidents fought in the Revolutionary War?

    A. 2   *C. 4*

    B. 3   *D. 7*

2. Which president was famous for the Battle of Tippecanoe?

    A. Zachary Taylor   *C. Dwight D. Eisenhower*

    B. William Henry Harrison   *D. Ulysses S. Grant*

3. Which president, when just a young boy, watched the Battle of Bunker Hill that was fought near his family farm?

    A. James Madison   *C. Franklin Pierce*

    B. James Garfield   *D. John Quincy Adams*

4. What future president was a part of the Rough Riders during the Spanish-American War?

A. *Grover Cleveland*   C. *Theodore Roosevelt*

B. *Chester Arthur*   D. *Abraham Lincoln*

5. Who was president when the U.S. invaded Panama and overthrew the dictator Noriega?

A. *Ronald Reagan*   C. *Theodore Roosevelt*

B. *George H.W. Bush*   D. *Dwight D. Eisenhower*

6. Which future president was Supreme Allied Commander of WWII?

A. *Dwight D. Eisenhower*   C. *George Washington*

B. *William McKinley*   D. *Harry Truman*

7. During the Mexican War, what future president barely escaped injury as a shot tore through his sleeve and another passed through the front of his coat taking off a button?

A. *Andrew Jackson*   C. *John Tyler*

B. *William H. Harrison*   D. *Zachary Taylor*

8. Which president was responsible for ending the Korean War?

A. *Franklin D. Roosevelt*   C. *John F. Kennedy*

B. *Dwight D. Eisenhower*   D. *Richard Nixon*

9. Which president was responsible for U.S. invading Iraq after convincing the American public that Iraq was in possession of weapons of mass destruction?

A. *George H.W. Bush*   C. *Bill Clinton*

B. *Barack Obama*   D. *George W. Bush*

10. Which president was responsible for the use of the atomic bomb against Japan to put an end to WWII?

A. *Harry Truman*   C. *Dwight D. Eisenhower*

B. *Franklin D. Roosevelt*   D. *Herbert Hoover*

11. Who was the last Civil War general to become president?

A. *Ulysses S. Grant*   C. *Zachary Taylor*

B. *Benjamin Harrison*   D. *William McKinley*

12. Which president had served in the army for four decades which included the War of 1812, Black Hawk War, and the second Seminole Wars?

A. *Abraham Lincoln*   C. *James Madison*

B. *William H. Harrison*   D. *Zachary Taylor*

13. In the War of 1812, which future president became a hero when he defeated the British at New Orleans?

A. *Andrew Jackson*   C. *Zachary Taylor*

B. *John Tyler*   D. *James Madison*

14. Which future president had opposed the use of the atomic bomb against Japan?

A. Harry Truman   C. Dwight D. Eisenhower

B. Franklin D. Roosevelt   D. John F. Kennedy

15. When this president took office, the war in Vietnam was costing Americans $60 – $80 million dollars a day and were losing the lives of approximately three hundred American soldiers a week. This president's main concern when he took office was to solve this issue. Who was he?

A. John F. Kennedy   C. Gerald Ford

B. Richard Nixon   D. Lyndon B. Johnson

16. What future president survived four plane crashes during WWII?

A. Dwight D. Eisenhower   C. George H.W. Bush

B. Ronald Reagan   D. Gerald Ford

17. Confederate General Robert E. Lee surrendered to this future president at Appomattox Court House in Virginia putting an end to the Civil War. Who was he?

A. Zachary Taylor   C. Abraham Lincoln

B. Andrew Johnson   D. Ulysses S. Grant

18. Which president stated detainees of terrorists were not protected by the Geneva Convention, and as a result many of the detainees were tortured?

A. Barack Obama   C. George H.W. Bush

B. Bill Clinton   D. George W. Bush

19. Which president along with his Secretary of State are considered the "founding fathers" of ISIS, the world's most brutal terrorist organization, by supporting the Syrian organization which was dominated by al Qaeda which morphed into what we today call ISIS?

A. Donald Trump   *C. Bill Clinton*

B. Barack Obama   *D. George H.W. Bush*

20. What future president was wounded during the American Revolutionary War?

A. James Monroe   *C. George Washington*

B. John Adams   *D. Andrew Jackson*

21. Can you name the four presidents who fought or served in the Revolutionary War?

A. G. Washington, J. Adams, J. Monroe, & A. Jackson

B. G. Washington, J. Madison, T. Jefferson, & A. Jackson

C. G. Washington, J. Madison, J. Monroe, & A. Jackson

D. G. Washington, J. Adams, J. Monroe, J. Quincy Adams

22. Which president won a Nobel Peace Prize for mediating the Russo-Japanese War?

A. Jimmy Carter   *C. Richard Nixon*

B. Franklin D. Roosevelt   *D. Theodore Roosevelt*

23. The Treaty of Versailles, which brought an end to WWI, was drafted

by the Big Four powers – those of the United States, Great Britain, France, and Italy. What U.S. president helped draft this treaty?

A. *Woodrow Wilson*   C. *Theodore Roosevelt*

B. *Harry Truman*   D. *William H. Taft*

24. What president received the Distinguished Flying Cross for bravery?

A. *George W. Bush*   C. *Dwight D. Eisenhower*

B. *George H.W. Bush*   D. *Jimmy Carter*

25. Who was president during the days when the world was on the brink of nuclear annihilation known as the Cuban Missile Crisis?

A. *Woodrow Wilson*   C. *Herbert Hoover*

B. *Calvin Coolidge*   D. *John F. Kennedy*

26. Which future president led the invasion known in history as D-Day?

A. *Franklin D. Roosevelt*   C. *Dwight D. Eisenhower*

B. *John F. Kennedy*   D. *George H.W. Bush*

27. How many presidents fought or served in the Civil War?

A. *2*   C. *5*

B. *4*   D. *8*

28. Who was president when the United States invaded Afghanistan to overthrow the Taliban government?

A. George H.W. Bush   C. Barack Obama

B. George W. Bush   D. Ronald Reagan

29. Which president led the U.S. into the Korean War?

A. Harry Truman   C. Calvin Coolidge

B. Dwight D. Eisenhower   D. Warren Harding

30. What future president, on Christmas night in the year 1776, led his men across the Delaware River and attacked the Hessian mercenaries?

A. George Washington   C. James Monroe

B. Andrew Jackson   D. James Madison

31. Which president led the nation into war with Spain over Cuban independence?

A. Theodore Roosevelt   C. William McKinley

B. Benjamin Harrison   D. Woodrow Wilson

32. A few weeks after he left the office of the presidency, Confederates fired on Ft. Sumter which was the beginning of the Civil War. Who was the president who had just left office?

A. James Buchanan   C. Franklin Pierce

B. Zachary Taylor   D. Abraham Lincoln

33. What future president was in the Navy and in a torpedo boat when it was rammed by a Japanese warship? This future president led the

survivors to a nearby island where they were later rescued.

A. Richard Nixon   C. John F. Kennedy

B. George H.W. Bush   D. Jimmy Carter

34. Who was president when British troops set fire to the White House and the Capitol?

A. James Monroe   C. Thomas Jefferson

B. James Madison   D. John Adams

35. Which future president was with George Washington and his troops at Valley Forge during the harsh winter of 1777 – 1778?

A. John Adams   C. Andrew Jackson

B. William H. Harrison   D. James Monroe

36. Which future president sent troops to China to help put an end to the Boxer Rebellion, an uprising against foreign intervention in China?

A. Herbert Hoover   C. William H. Taft

B. William McKinley   D. Benjamin Harrison

37. During WWII this future president's plane was hit and on fire, but he continued on and successfully bombed his target before ejecting out of his plane. He was rescued in the water by an American submarine. Who was he?

A. George H.W. Bush   C. Bill Clinton

B. John F. Kennedy   D. George W. Bush

38. Which future president was appointed Commander-in-Chief of the Colonial forces against Great Britain?

A. Dwight D. Eisenhower   *C. Ulysses S. Grant*

B. William H. Harrison   *D. George Washington*

39. Which president was a general and a hero in the Mexican-American War and the War of 1812?

A. James Polk   *C. Zachary Taylor*

B. Theodore Roosevelt   *D. Andrew Jackson*

40. At the beginning of WWI what president declared America neutral, but by 1917 he asked Congress to declare war when Germany sunk American ships and ignored U.S. neutrality? Who was he?

A. Woodrow Wilson   *C. Franklin D. Roosevelt*

B. William H. Taft   *D. Calvin Coolidge*

41. What future president fought in the Revolutionary War when he was a teenager?

A. Thomas Jefferson   *C. James Madison*

B. James Monroe   *D. Andrew Jackson*

42. What future president commanded the Union Army during the Civil War?

A. Abraham Lincoln   *C. Ulysses S. Grant*

B. Franklin Pierce   *D. Benjamin Harrison*

43. Which president created an air lift to get supplies to the people of Berlin when the Russians blockaded western areas of Berlin?

A. Harry Truman

C. Herbert Hoover

B. Calvin Coolidge

D. Warren Harding

44. In 1863, what president reshaped the cause of the war from keeping the union intact to abolishing slavery?

A. Ulysses S. Grant

C. Zachary Taylor

B. James Polk

D. Abraham Lincoln

45. The day after Pearl Harbor was bombed by the Japanese, which president declared war on Japan?

A. Theodore Roosevelt

C. Herbert Hoover

B. Harry Truman

D. Franklin D. Roosevelt

46. What future president had winter quarters in the year 1777 at Valley Forge during the Revolutionary War?

A. James Madison

C. Andrew Jackson

B. George Washington

D. James Monroe

47. Who was the only president who had been a prisoner of war?

A. George Washington

C. Andrew Jackson

B. Ulysses S. Grant

D. John F. Kennedy

48. Which future president enlisted in the Black Hawk War and seeing no action, after leaving the military made the joke that the only blood he lost in the war was to mosquitoes?

A. Zachary Taylor

C. Benjamin Harrison

B. Abraham Lincoln

D. Millard Fillmore

49. Which president declared war which was known as Operation Desert Storm or the Persian Gulf War?

A. George H.W. Bush

C. Ronald Reagan

B. Dwight D. Eisenhower

D. George W. Bush

50. What future president served as a military aide to General Douglas MacArthur?

A. John F. Kennedy

C. George H.W. Bush

B. Theodore Roosevelt

D. Dwight D. Eisenhower

Answers

Chapter 15 - War Hawks and War Doves

1. C – Four

2. B - William H. Harrison

3. D - John Quincy Adams

4. C - Theodore Roosevelt

5. B - George H.W. Bush

6. A - Dwight D. Eisenhower

7. D - Zachary Taylor

8. B - Dwight D. Eisenhower

9. D - George W. Bush

10. A - Harry Truman

11. B - Benjamin Harrison

12. D - Zachary Taylor

13. A - Andrew Jackson

14. C - Dwight D. Eisenhower

15. B - Richard Nixon

16. C - George H.W. Bush

17. D - Ulysses S. Grant

18. D - George W. Bush

19. B - Barack Obama

Secretary of State Hillary Clinton was equally responsible.

20. A - James Monroe

21.C - George Washington, James Madison, James Monroe, and Andrew Jackson

22. D - Theodore Roosevelt

23. A - Woodrow Wilson

24. B - George H.W. Bush

25. D - John F. Kennedy

26. C - Dwight D. Eisenhower

27. D - 8

Andrew Johnson, Ulysses S. Grant, Rutherford B. Hayes, James Garfield, Chester Arthur, Benjamin Harrison, William McKinley, and Millard Fillmore

28. B - George W. Bush

29. A - Harry Truman

30. A - George Washington

31. C - William McKinley

The end result was U.S. possession over Puerto Rico, Guam, and the Philippines.

32. A - James Buchanan

33. C - John F. Kennedy

34. B - James Madison

35. D - James Monroe

36. B - William McKinley

37. A - George H.W. Bush

38. D - George Washington

39. C - Zachary Taylor

40. A - Woodrow Wilson

41. B - James Monroe

42. C - Ulysses S. Grant

43. A - Harry Truman

44. D - Abraham Lincoln

45. D - Franklin D. Roosevelt

President Roosevelt actually stated his reason on why we should declare war before a joint session of Congress and then did declare war on Japan.

46. B - George Washington

47. C - Andrew Jackson

He was taken prisoner by British soldiers when they invaded the Carolinas. While prisoner he refused to shine an officer's boots, the officer then hit Jackson across the face with his saber leaving a scar.

48. B - Abraham Lincoln

49. A - George H.W. Bush

50. D - Dwight D. Eisenhower

16

For This I Will Be Remembered

Answers are given on page 141 - 142.

1. Which president signed legislation establishing Yellowstone National Park, the nation's first national park?

   A. Ulysses S. Grant   *C. Theodore Roosevelt*

   B. Chester Arthur   *D. Benjamin Harrison*

2. Which president announced a plan to develop and build space based weapons to protect American soil against Soviet nuclear missiles?

   A. John F. Kennedy   *C. Dwight D. Eisenhower*

   B. George H.W. Bush   *D. Ronald Reagan*

3. Which president introduced the program Medicare?

   A. Herbert Hoover   *C. Lyndon B. Johnson*

   B. Franklin D. Roosevelt   *D. Harry Truman*

4. Which president supported the Lewis and Clark Expedition?

A. James Madison

C. John Quincy Adams

B. James Monroe

D. Thomas Jefferson

5. Which president gained popularity when he stood up to Khrushchev who people considered a Soviet bully?

A. John F. Kennedy

C. Ronald Reagan

B. Richard Nixon

D. Lyndon B. Johnson

6. Which president declared war on global terrorism?

A. Donald Trump

C. George W. Bush

B. Barack Obama

D. Bill Clinton

7. Which president fought to have the Panama Canal built?

A. Theodore Roosevelt

C. Dwight D. Eisenhower

B. Grover Cleveland

D. William H. Taft

8. Which president set the precedent for a limit of two terms as president?

A. Franklin D. Roosevelt

C. Abraham Lincoln

B. Thomas Jefferson

D. George Washington

9. Which president created the Federal Reserve?

A. William McKinley

C. Harry Truman

B. *Woodrow Wilson*   D. *William H. Taft*

10. Which president vetoed the most bills?

A. *Grover Cleveland*   C. *William H. Taft*

B. *Barack Obama*   D. *Calvin Coolidge*

11. One of this president's main objectives was to focus on Reconstruction. Who was he?

A. *Abraham Lincoln*   C. *Ulysses S. Grant*

B. *Andrew Johnson*   D. *James Garfield*

12. Which president appointed more women to federal posts than any other president?

A. *Harry Truman*   C. *Woodrow Wilson*

B. *Franklin D. Roosevelt*   D. *John F. Kennedy*

13. Which president worked at alleviating poverty and creating a 'Great Society' for all Americans?

A. *John F. Kennedy*   C. *Thomas Jefferson*

B. *Herbert Hoover*   D. *Lyndon B. Johnson*

14. On his last day in office which president signed a bill making Florida the 27th state?

A. *John Tyler*   C. *James Polk*

B. *Andrew Johnson*   D. *Grover Cleveland*

15. Which president was the driving force between the alliance between the U.S., Great Britain, and the Soviet Union which brought about the United Nations?

A. *Harry Truman*   C. *Woodrow Wilson*

B. *Dwight D. Eisenhower*   D. *Franklin D. Roosevelt*

16. Which president appointed Sandra Day O'Connor as the first woman in the U.S. Supreme Court?

A. *Jimmy Carter*   C. *George H.W. Bush*

B. *Ronald Reagan*   D. *Richard Nixon*

17. During whose presidency did his Secretary of State, William Seward, negotiate with Russia for the purchase of Alaska?

A. *Andrew Jackson*   C. *Andrew Johnson*

B. *Martin Van Buren*   D. *James Polk*

18. Same sex marriage was passed during which president's administration?

A. *Barack Obama*   C. *Bill Clinton*

B. *George W. Bush*   D. *Ronald Reagan*

19. Which president launched the Space Race?

A. *Dwight D. Eisenhower*   C. *John F. Kennedy*

B. Richard Nixon   D. Ronald Reagan

20. Which president signed into law a bill recognizing squatter's rights to occupy public lands?

A. Grover Cleveland   C. Millard Fillmore

B. John Tyler   D. William H. Harrison

21. Who was president at the time Congress overrode a president on a bill that the president had vetoed?

A. Barack Obama   C. Warren Harding

B. Bill Clinton   D. Andrew Johnson

22. Who was president when the Erie Canal was completed?

A. John Quincy Adams   C. Ulysses S. Grant

B. Martin Van Buren   D. Grover Cleveland

23. Which president's foreign policy allowed the U.S. to have an active role in world affairs?

A. Theodore Roosevelt   C. Calvin Coolidge

B. William McKinley   D. Woodrow Wilson

24. Which president fought hard against special favors to any economic groups? He stated the reason for this was that, "Federal Aid encourages the expectation of paternal care on the part of the government and weakens the sturdiness of our national character"?

A. *Ronald Reagan*   C. *Grover Cleveland*

B. *Thomas Jefferson*   D. *Calvin Coolidge*

25. Which president took up the cause of the Clean Power Plan which was aimed at reducing greenhouse gas emissions, which he considered an important move against climate change?

A. *George W. Bush*   C. *Jimmy Carter*

B. *Barack Obama*   D. *Bill Clinton*

Answers

Chapter 16 – For This I Will Be Remembered

1. A - Ulysses S. Grant

2. D - Ronald Reagan

3. C - Lyndon B. Johnson

4. D - Thomas Jefferson

5. B - Richard Nixon

6. C - George W. Bush

7. A - Theodore Roosevelt

8. D - George Washington

9. B - Woodrow Wilson

10. A - Grover Cleveland

11. C - Ulysses S. Grant

12. B - Franklin D. Roosevelt

13. D - Lyndon B. Johnson

14. A - John Tyler

15. D - Franklin D. Roosevelt

16. B - Ronald Reagan

17. C - Andrew Johnson

Alaska was purchased from Russia for $7 million. At the time critics called it 'Seward's Folly' thinking the purchase was a mistake.

18. A - Barack Obama

19. A - Dwight D. Eisenhower

20. B - John Tyler

People who settled on and improved unsurveyed public land were entitled to first purchase rights.

21. D – Andrew Johnson

22. A - John Quincy Adams

23. B - William McKinley

24. C - Grover Cleveland

25. B - Barack Obama

17

Name The President

Answers are given on pages 152 - 154.

1. Which president was a peanut farmer?

    A. Lyndon B. Johnson   *C. Ronald Reagan*

    B. Andrew Johnson   *D. Jimmy Carter*

2. Which president secretly sent Iran, a country in which the United States has no diplomatic relations, $400 million *in cash* which resulted in charges by the American public of violating a U.S. practice not to pay for hostages and in doing so empowering a major source of terrorism?

    A. George H.W. Bush   *C. George W. Bush*

    B. Barack Obama   *D. Bill Clinton*

3. Which president is the only president to have had his father administer the presidential oath of office to him?

    A. George W. Bush   *C. Calvin Coolidge*

    B. Franklin D. Roosevelt   *D. John Quincy Adams*

4. Who has been our richest president to date?

A. Thomas Jefferson   C. John F. Kennedy

B. Franklin D. Roosevelt   D. Donald Trump

5. Which two presidents died on the same day, the 50th Anniversary of the Declaration of Independence in 1826?

A. G. Washington & T. Jefferson   C. J. Adams & T. Jefferson

B. J. Madison & J. Monroe   D. T. Jefferson & J. Madison

6. Who is the only president buried in Washington?

A. John F. Kennedy   C. George Washington

B. Woodrow Wilson   D. Abraham Lincoln

7. How were the two presidents Theodore Roosevelt and Franklin Roosevelt related?

A. Cousins   C. Brothers-in-law

B. Brothers   D. Grandfather & Grandson

8. Which was the last president who was born a British subject?

A. Martin Van Buren   C. James Monroe

B. John Tyler   D. William Henry Harrison

9. Which sitting president accused the mainstream media of reporting "fake news" when they clearly reported their biased opinions and rumors rather than the news?

A. Bill Clinton   C. Donald Trump

B. Barack Obama   D. George W. Bush

10. Which president was an indentured servant who ran away?

A. James Monroe   C. John Tyler

B. Zachary Taylor   D. Andrew Johnson

11. Which president had several inventions?

A. Abraham Lincoln   C. Thomas Jefferson

B. Theodore Roosevelt   D. Herbert Hoover

12. Which president often made his own breakfast in the White House?

A. Gerald Ford   C. Woodrow Wilson

B. Lyndon B. Johnson   D. George W. Bush

13. Was Abraham Lincoln a Democrat or Republican?

A. Democrat   B. Republican

14. Which vice-president was visiting his father, when in the middle of the night he was informed that the president was dead? He was sworn in to the office of the presidency by his father by candlelight and then went back to sleep.

A. John Adams   C. Calvin Coolidge

B. John Tyler   D. Millard Fillmore

15. Who was the first president to marry while president?

    A. John Tyler   *C. Martin Van Buren*

    B. James Buchanan   *D. Woodrow Wilson*

16. In the presidential election of the year 2000, it was the United States Supreme Court who finally determined who the next president would be. Who did they decide won the office of the presidency?

    A. Gerald Ford   *C. George W. Bush*

    B. Bill Clinton   *D. George H.W. Bush*

17. Which president gave President Nixon a full pardon?

    A. George H.W. Bush   *C. Lyndon B. Johnson*

    B. Jimmy Carter   *D. Gerald Ford*

18. What president hated political partisanship and felt that leaders should be able to discuss important issues without being bound by party loyalty?

    A. Donald Trump   *C. Ronald Reagan*

    B. George Washington   *D. James Monroe*

19. Which president delivered the longest inaugural address, lasting one hour and forty minutes?

    A. John Adams   *C. William Henry Harrison*

    B. Martin Van Buren   *D. George Washington*

20. Which president wrote his own epitaph and never even mentioned that he had been president?

A. Thomas Jefferson

C. James Monroe

B. Ulysses S. Grant

D. Dwight D. Eisenhower

21. Courtesy has always been that a former president is never seen or heard criticizing his successors, therefore preserving the integrity of the office. Which president after leaving office not only didn't leave Washington, D.C. but was vocal about the incoming president's actions and worked behind his back to undermine his presidency?

A. John Adams

C. Lyndon B. Johnson

B. Dwight D. Eisenhower

D. Barack Obama

22. Which president never attended a single day of school?

A. Abraham Lincoln

C. Zachary Taylor

B. Andrew Johnson

D. Franklin Pierce

23. Before becoming president he was a sheriff, public executioner, and personally hung two murderers. Who was he?

A. Andrew Johnson

C. Benjamin Harrison

B. Grover Cleveland

D. William H. Taft

24. Which president talked to astronauts on the moon from the White House by using a radio-telephone?

A. John F. Kennedy

C. Richard Nixon

B. *George H.W. Bush*   D. *Lyndon B. Johnson*

25. In warm weather which president went skinny-dipping in the Potomac early in the morning?

A. *John Quincy Adams*   C. *George Washington*

B. *Andrew Jackson*   D. *James Polk*

26. Which president started the tradition of throwing out the first ball for the opening of baseball season?

A. *William Howard Taft*   C. *Calvin Coolidge*

B. *George W. Bush*   D. *Woodrow Wilson*

27. Who was the first Republican to be elected to the Presidency?

A. *George Washington*   C. *Thomas Jefferson*

B. *Abraham Lincoln*   D. *Theodore Roosevelt*

28. Which president's heads are depicted on Mt. Rushmore?

A. *Washington, Jefferson, Lincoln, T. Roosevelt*

B. *Washington, Jefferson, Madison, Lincoln,*

C. *Washington, Jefferson, Lincoln, F. Roosevelt*

D. *Washington, Jefferson, Lincoln, Reagan*

29. Who was the oldest man to be inaugurated as president?

A. Donald Trump

B. Ronald Reagan

C. George H.W. Bush

D. Lyndon B. Johnson

30. Which president is the only president to have a patent in his name?

A. Abraham Lincoln

B. Millard Fillmore

C. Barack Obama

D. Thomas Jefferson

31. Which president was scouted by more than one professional baseball team while still a high school student?

A. George W. Bush

B. Gerald Ford

C. Donald Trump

D. George H.W. Bush

32. Which president was the last president of the Founding Fathers?

A. George Washington

B. John Quincy Adams

C. Thomas Jefferson

D. James Monroe

33. His approval ratings dropped significantly when it was found the IRS was targeting conservative organizations and also due to the cover up of the Benghazi terrorist killings. Who was he?

A. George W. Bush

B. Lyndon B. Johnson

C. Barack Obama

D. Bill Clinton

34. Which president hated cats and after retiring would shoot at any cats that came near his home?

A. John Adams   C. Lyndon B. Johnson

B. Calvin Coolidge   D. Dwight D. Eisenhower

35. Which president served the shortest term of presidency?

A. William H. Harrison   C. James Garfield

B. Zachary Taylor   D. James Buchanan

36. Which president studied nuclear physics?

A. Herbert Hoover   C. Jimmy Carter

B. Harry Truman   D. Woodrow Wilson

37. Which president signed into legislation for the founding of the Smithsonian Institution as an establishment dedicated to the "increase and diffusion of knowledge" ?

A. James Polk   C. Thomas Jefferson

B. James Buchanan   D. Rutherford B. Hayes

38. Which two presidents signed the Constitution?

A. G. Washington & J. Madison   C. G. Washington & J. Adams

B. T. Jefferson & J. Monroe   D. J. Adams & T. Jefferson

39. Which two presidents signed the Declaration of Independence?

A. G. Washington & T. Jefferson   C. G. Washington & J. Adams

B. *J. Adams & T. Jefferson*   D. *J. Adams & J. Monroe*

40. Which president has a star on the Hollywood Walk of Fame?

   A. *John F. Kennedy*   C. *Ronald Reagan*

   B. *Bill Clinton*   D. *Donald Trump*

Answers

Chapter 17 – Name The President

1. D - Jimmy Carter

2. B - Barack Obama

3. C - Calvin Coolidge

4. D - Donald Trump

5. C - John Adams and Thomas Jefferson

6. B - Woodrow Wilson

 If you were thinking of John F. Kennedy and William H. Taft who are buried at Arlington National Cemetery, that is actually located in Virginia. Woodrow Wilson was buried at Washington Cathedral in Washington, D.C.

7. A - They were cousins.

8. D - William Henry Harrison

9. C - Donald Trump

10. D - Andrew Johnson

 Many children from poor families were sold into indentured servitude. When he was twelve years old, he escaped from his master, a tailor in North Carolina.

11. C - Thomas Jefferson

12. A - Gerald Ford

13. B - Republican

14. C - Calvin Coolidge

15. A - John Tyler

His first wife died while he was president. He remarried while still in office.

16. C - George W Bush

* *The United States Supreme Court resolved the dispute in the 2000 presidential election determining that George W. Bush won the presidency.*

17. D - Gerald Ford

18. B - George Washington.

He was unable to put a stop to political parties.

19. C - William Henry Harrison

The shortest inaugural address was given by George Washington which consisted of only 133 words.

20. A - Thomas Jefferson

21. D – Barack Obama

22. B - Andrew Johnson

23. B - Grover Cleveland

24. C - Richard Nixon

25. A - John Quincy Adams

The last time he went skinny-dipping in the Potomac River he was seventy nine years old.

26. A - William Howard Taft

27. B - Abraham Lincoln

28. A - George Washington, Thomas Jefferson, Abraham Lincoln, and Theodore Roosevelt

29. B - Ronald Reagan

30. A - Abraham Lincoln

31. C - Donald Trump

While still a high school student he was scouted by both the Phillies and the Boston Red Sox.

32. D - James Monroe

33. C - Barack Obama

34. D - Dwight D. Eisenhower

35. A - William H. Harrison

He died thirty two days after elected. His inaugural address lasted almost two hours in which time he stood in the bad weather wearing no hat or coat. After his inaugural address he attended a round of receptions in his wet clothing and developed a chill which within days turned into a cold and then progressed into pneumonia. One month after taking office he passed away.

36. C - Jimmy Carter

37. A - James Polk

38. A - George Washington & James Madison

39. B – John Adams & Thomas Jefferson

40. D - Donald Trump

18

Airing Their Dirty Laundry

Answers are given on page 165 - 168.

1. Which president had extramarital affairs and left behind love letters to a mistress which were considered crude to the point of being vulgar and are now available to see at the Library of Congress?

A. John F. Kennedy   *C. Warren Harding*

B. Donald Trump   *D. Bill Clinton*

2. Who was president during the cover-up of the attack on the American consulate in Benghazi where four U.S. nationals were killed in the attack?

A. Bill Clinton   *C. George W. Bush*

B. Barack Obama   *D. Richard Nixon*

3. Which president was accused of leaving his dog behind after a family vacation and then sent a Navy destroyer, at tax payers expense, to rescue the dog?

A. Franklin D. Roosevelt   *C. Warren Harding*

B. Calvin Coolidge   *D. George H.W. Bush*

4. Which president had the scandal of being accused of agreeing with McCarthyism during his term of office due to his silence on the matter?

A. John F. Kennedy

C. Calvin Coolidge

B. Harry Truman

D. Dwight D. Eisenhower

5. Which president ordered American forces to occupy the Philippines where a brutal war broke out against the Philippine Republic? This decision was radically opposed by American citizens to the point that they offered to purchase the Philippines to give them their independence.

A. William McKinley

C. William H. Taft

B. Theodore Roosevelt

D. Chester Arthur

6. Which president in his bachelor days was accused of rape, impregnating a woman, and then having her baby kidnapped and adopted without her consent?

A. James Polk

C. Bill Clinton

B. Andrew Johnson

D. Grover Cleveland

7. Which president's administration was considered to be the most corrupt with two major scandals, The Whiskey Ring Scandal and the Credit Mobilier Scandal occurring during his presidency?

A. Warren Harding

C. Ulysses S. Grant

B. Andrew Johnson

D. Rutherford B. Hayes

8. Which president had several mistresses, even leaving one of them half of his $3 million estate?

A. John F. Kennedy

C. John Quincy Adams

B. Franklin D. Roosevelt

D. Lyndon B. Johnson

9. Which president drank alcohol in the White House, which at that time was a violation of the Eighteenth Amendment?

A. Warren Harding

C. Rutherford B. Hayes

B. Grover Cleveland

D. Calvin Coolidge

10. Congress was a constant thorn in his side during his entire presidency due to the fact that he was the first vice-president to become president after the death of his predecessor. Congress did not want him in office and they made it as difficult for him as possible. In retaliation, the president counteracted by vetoing several pieces of legislation. Which president was this?

A. John Tyler

C. Andrew Johnson

B. Chester Arthur

D. Lyndon B. Johnson

11. During his presidency the IRS was used to illegally abuse and target his political opponents and when exposed federal investigations and congressional oversight were obstructed and protected. Who was this president?

A. Donald Trump

C. Barack Obama

B. Bill Clinton

D. George H.W. Bush

12. Which president's reputation and respect suffered due to his ties with members of organized crime and his womanizing ways?

A. Lyndon B. Johnson

C. Bill Clinton

B. *John F. Kennedy*   D. *Franklin D. Roosevelt*

13. Which president had an affair with his wife's social secretary?

   A. *John F. Kennedy*   C. *Bill Clinton*

   B. *Jimmy Carter*   D. *Franklin D. Roosevelt*

14. Which president was accused of having illegitimate children with one of his slaves, which just years ago was confirmed by DNA testing?

   A. *John Tyler*   C. *Thomas Jefferson*

   B. *George Washington*   D. *William H. Harrison*

15. The scandal of the Monica Lewinsky affair was at first denied by this president. This president was impeached for perjury and obstruction of justice but remained in office. Who was he?

   A. *Richard Nixon*   C. *Barack Obama*

   B. *John F. Kennedy*   D. *Bill Clinton*

16. Which president has been married three times, and his young children from his first marriage learned of their father's extra-marital affair in the tabloid headlines?

   A. *John F. Kennedy*   C. *Donald Trump*

   B. *John Tyler*   D. *Franklin D. Roosevelt*

17. Which president leaves behind a path of destruction with stories of murder of those who have crossed the president and first lady?

A. Donald Trump

B. Herbert Hoover

C. Zachary Taylor

D. Bill Clinton

18. Which president was known to have romantic trysts with his mistress in the closet in the presidential office and had an illegitimate daughter with her that he refused to ever lay eyes on?

A. Lyndon B. Johnson

B. Warren Harding

C. Donald Trump

D. Bill Clinton

19. Which president gave former President Nixon an unconditional pardon for his involvement in Watergate, which both political parties were opposed to?

A. John F. Kennedy

B. Jimmy Carter

C. George H.W. Bush

D. Gerald Ford

20. Which president, along with his brother, was having an affair with the actress Marilyn Monroe who was found dead after having threatened to come forward about the president's infidelities?

A. John F. Kennedy

B. Bill Clinton

C. Lyndon B. Johnson

D. Donald Trump

21. Which of our presidents left office in disgrace over the Watergate Scandal?

A. Ronald Reagan

B. Jimmy Carter

C. Bill Clinton

D. Barack Obama

22. Who was president when the Department of Justice told the FBI director to *'stand down'* in his investigation of a former First Lady who was at the time running for the presidency? This appeared to have the backing of the president, considering the fact that when interviewed the president stated before the investigation was completed that there had been no crime committed.

A. Donald Trump

C. John F. Kennedy

B. Barack Obama

D. Andrew Johnson

23. Which president was accused of sexual misconduct and rape? He was confronted by his accusers when his own wife, a former First Lady, was herself running for the presidency.

A. Grover Cleveland

C. Bill Clinton

B. Donald Trump

D. Franklin D. Roosevelt

24. Which president sent his mistress a ticket to his inauguration?

A. John F. Kennedy

C. Lyndon B. Johnson

B. Franklin D. Roosevelt

D. Bill Clinton

25. Which president had to live with the controversy of his decision to buy the Panama Canal from the French, a decision that was adamantly opposed by Congress, and then organized a revolution overthrowing the government of Panama?

A. Franklin D. Roosevelt

C. Theodore Roosevelt

B. William McKinley

D. James Garfield

26. Which president was involved in the Star Route Scandal, a scheme where postal officials received bribes in exchange for giving postal delivery contracts to southern areas?

    A. James Garfield   *C. Andrew Johnson*

    B. Jimmy Carter   *D. John Tyler*

27. Who was president during the Iran-Contra Scandal, where money obtained from selling arms to Iran was secretly passed on to the revolutionary Contras in Nicaragua?

    A. Jimmy Carter   *C. Gerald Ford*

    B. Ronald Reagan   *D. George H.W. Bush*

28. Which president's administration was involved with speculation in the gold market driving up the price of gold which adversely affected those who had invested in gold?

    A. Martin Van Buren   *C. Benjamin Harrison*

    B. Chester Arthur   *D. Ulysses S. Grant*

29. Which president surprisingly was corruption free as a president, yet in his days before the presidency he had been tossed out of other political offices due to corruption?

    A. Chester Arthur   *C. Warren Harding*

    B. Ulysses S. Grant   *D. Theodore Roosevelt*

30. Which president was involved in the Watergate scandal, which is considered to be the most notorious presidential scandal to date?

A. Gerald Ford   C. Richard Nixon

B. Harry Truman   D. Jimmy Carter

31. Which president was accused by the mainstream media, with no evidence to collaborate their accusations, that the president colluded with Russia during the presidential election?

A. Bill Clinton   C. John F. Kennedy

B. Donald Trump   D. George W. Bush

32. Which president was condemned for his handling of the Great Depression and to further blacken his name was responsible for turning Army troops out to break up a protest of WWI veterans who had assembled in Washington to demand more pay that they had been previously promised?

A. Franklin D. Roosevelt   C. Harry Truman

B. Andrew Johnson   D. Herbert Hoover

33. Which president, after leaving office, was discovered to have lied to the American people about America's actions during the Vietnam War?

A. John F. Kennedy   C. Dwight D. Eisenhower

B. Lyndon B. Johnson   D. Richard Nixon

34. Which president appeared weak in his actions when 52 American hostages were taken in Tehran and failed to secure their release during his presidency?

A. Ronald Reagan   C. Jimmy Carter

B. Gerald Ford   D. Barack Obama

35. Which president has been accused of fathering a black son whose mother was a prostitute?

A. Warren Harding   C. Grover Cleveland

B. Andrew Johnson   D. Bill Clinton

36. Which president was discovered to have spied on the incoming president and leaked information, both during his presidential campaign and after he was elected, along with spying on American citizens and political opponents?

A. Barack Obama   C. Bill Clinton

B. Donald Trump   D. Richard Nixon

37. Which former president has been accused of being involved in a "pay-to-play" scheme in which foreign governments could donate money to the president's foundation in exchange for beneficial treatment from the government influenced by the former president and former first lady who at the time was the Secretary of State with plans to run for the presidency?

A. Bill Clinton   C. Barack Obama

B. George W. Bush   D. Jimmy Carter

38. When the Supreme Court ruled on the Dred Scott case, which president was discovered to have contacted and pressured one of the Justices from his state to change his vote to support the president's stance on the issue?

A. *Franklin Pierce*   C. *Rutherford B. Hayes*

B. *James Buchanan*   D. *James Garfield*

39. Which president in a poker game lost a set of White House china dating from the days of Benjamin Harrison?

A. *Richard Nixon*   C. *Warren Harding*

B. *Ulysses S. Grant*   D. *Grover Cleveland*

40. Which president has had to deal with leaks within his own office and those who work closely to him?

A. *George W. Bush*   C. *Richard Nixon*

B. *Donald Trump*   D. *Ronald Reagan*

Answers

Chapter 18 – Airing Their Dirty Laundry

1. C - Warren Harding

The letters were written before he became president but he was making blackmail payments from American taxpayers to the recipient of the letters while president.

2. B - Barack Obama

3. A - Franklin D. Roosevelt

4. D – Dwight D. Eisenhower

5. A - William McKinley

6. D - Grover Cleveland

7. C – Ulysses S. Grant

8. B - Franklin D. Roosevelt

9. A - Warren Harding

10. A - John Tyler

11. C - Barack Obama

12. B - John F. Kennedy

13. D - Franklin D. Roosevelt

When his wife discovered the affair she gave him an ultimatum – stop seeing the other woman or she would divorce him. He agreed to stop seeing the woman, but continued seeing her for the rest of his life. She was by his side when he died.

14. C - Thomas Jefferson

*   *It was rumored for over two hundred years that Thomas Jefferson had illegitimate children with his slave Sally Hemings. DNA tests were completed and after careful study and consideration of all the facts presented, The Thomas Jefferson Foundation Research Committee concluded that there was a "high probability that Thomas Jefferson was the father of Eston Hemings, and that he was likely the father of all six of her children."*

Other presidents also accused of having had illegitimate children

William H. Harrison *also was said to have had children with one of his slaves.*

John Tyler *also was rumored to have at least one child with a slave, but has not been proven one way or the other.*

Grover Cleveland. *There are two stories about this: One is that the mother of his illegitimate child threatened to go to the authorities due to Grover raping her which resulted in the child. He threatened her life and had her placed in a mental asylum, where she was soon let go after it was determined she wasn't crazy, but instead it was determined she had a politician out to destroy her to cover up his own actions. The other story was she was a mistress that he had a consensual affair with and the child was a result of this affair. The child was taken and given up for adoption without the mother's consent.*

Warren Harding *had an illegitimate child with a mistress proven by DNA.*

Only Thomas Jefferson's and Warren Harding's illegitimate children have been proven through DNA testing. The other presidents are rumors that have not been substantiated.

15. D - Bill Clinton

*   *It later came out that Monica Lewinsky wasn't the only one that pointed the finger at him about his sexual activities.*

16. C – Donald Trump

17. D - Bill Clinton

18. C - Warren Harding

DNA findings proved that he was indeed the father of the child even though throughout his lifetime he denied it.

19. D - Gerald Ford

20. A – John F. Kennedy

Official reports state her death as suicide, but there have always been rumors that the Kennedys had something to do with her death to protect their image.

21. D - Richard Nixon

22. B - Barack Obama

23. C - Bill Clinton

24. B - Franklin D. Roosevelt

25. C - Theodore Roosevelt

His daughter Ethel years after her father's death supported the proposed revision of the Panama Canal Treaty

26. A - James Garfield

27. B - Ronald Reagan

28. D - Ulysses S. Grant

29. A - Chester Arthur

30. C - Richard Nixon

31. B - Donald Trump

32. D – Herbert Hoover

33. B - Lyndon B. Johnson

34. C - Jimmy Carter

35. D - Bill Clinton

To date this has not been proved or disproved as the president refuses to have DNA testing done.

36. A - Barack Obama

37. A - Bill Clinton

38. B - James Buchanan

39. C - Warren Harding

40. B - Donald Trump

19

Presidential Perks

Answers are given on page 173 - 175.

1. There has been a presidential yacht, or floating White House, since 1880. Critics crying abuse of taxpayer's money and upset by the expense of the annual upkeep expenses were incentive for which president to sell the presidential yacht sold in 1977?

   A. Dwight D. Eisenhower   *C. Gerald Ford*

   B. Lyndon B. Johnson   *D. Jimmy Carter*

2. One of the perks of a president is to live in the White House, within it's 132 rooms and 35 bathrooms with a personal movie screen room, swimming pool, basketball courts, putting green, and staff to wait on you hand and foot. One perk the presidential family doesn't have that is paid for out of their own pocket is what?

   A. Maid service   *C. Grocery bills*

   B. Travel expenses   *D. Medical bills*

3. One of the perks of the president is the South Lawn, which is quite extensive. Many presidents enjoying their sports have their own sports areas designed and implemented, such as a putting green, swimming

pool, basketball courts, or tennis courts. Which president had an outdoor swimming pool built?

A. Jimmy Carter

C. Calvin Coolidge

B. Gerald Ford

D. John F. Kennedy

4. A presidential perk for presidents is never having to drive in traffic, or anywhere. By the time they leave office some presidents haven't been behind the wheel for 8 years or more. Who was the first president to enjoy the perk of being driven in a special built armored limousine?

A. Franklin D. Roosevelt

C. William McKinley

B. Theodore Roosevelt

D. Woodrow Wilson

5. Many presidents have enjoyed the perk of spending time at Camp David, a secluded presidential retreat with cabins, swimming pool, skeet shooting, hiking trails, and bowling alley. Which president named the resort Camp David after his grandson?

A. Theodore Roosevelt

C. Dwight D. Eisenhower

B. Jimmy Carter

D. William H. Taft

6. Which presidential family cost the taxpayers the most in their use of Air Force One – both for presidential use, family vacations, and personal use?

A. George W. Bush

C. Donald Trump

B. Barack Obama

D. Bill Clinton

7. Presidents are protected by the Secret Service during their time in

office, but after they retire how are they protected?

A. Lifetime security by Secret Service for presidents, wives, & children until the age of 16

B. Secret Service for presidents & first ladies for up to 10 years after they leave office

C. Secret Service for 10 years and after that the president can pay out of pocket for continued security as he deems necessary

D. Private security hired to protect the president, but not his family, for 5 years after leaving office and after that out of his own pocket

8. Which of these perks *doesn't* a president get?

A. Free barber, medical care, food taster to be sure his food isn't poisoned while out of the White House

B. After retiring: security for the remainder of his life, presidential library, use of the Blair House

C. A steward that travels with them to prepare their food, maid service, florist, entertainment budget

D. Access to any movie, lifetime use of Camp David, use of Air Force 2 after retiring, gifts sent from worldwide from the time they are in office

9. While a president does get a salary, there are several other perks that are much more lucrative not only during the presidency but after. How much is Donald Trump's salary as president?

A. $200,000   *C. $500,000*

B. $400,000   *D. $750,000*

10. Which of the items listed below, is *not* a perk the president receives?

A. Free M&M's, Coke & Pepsi   C. Choice of artwork

B. Funds to redecorate   D. Designer's clothing

Answers

Chapter 19 – Presidential Perks

1. D – Jimmy Carter

  * *As early as 1880 the presidents were able to enjoy what was called "The Floating White House," the presidential yacht. The purpose of the yacht was to escape the pressures of the executive office, recreation, and to entertain esteemed guests and was often used to carry out presidential business. Critics often complained of the excess and expense of this presidential perk and following through with a campaign promise President Jimmy Carter sold the presidential yacht in 1977. At that time the annual upkeep was costing taxpayers to the tune of $250,000. Elvis Presley was one of the owners after the sale of the yacht.*

2. C – Grocery bills (other than state dinners)

  * *Many presidents and First Ladies are surprised when first presented with a monthly bill for their food expenses (other than state dinners). This bill is paid out of pocket. Rosalynn Carter was one of the First Ladies upset by this revelation. When discovered they were responsible for their food bills she asked to be served leftovers and for the chefs to serve frugal meals. Another frugal First Lady was Mamie Eisenhower who was notorious for clipping coupons to save money.*

3. B – Gerald Ford

  * *Gerald Ford was one of the most athletic presidents and had an outdoor swimming pool put in so he could enjoy a daily swim. First Son Jack Ford took scuba lessons in the pool. It wasn't however the first White House swimming pool. In 1933, Franklin D. Roosevelt had an indoor pool built for therapy for his polio. John Kennedy also enjoyed the pool which helped his back. Even Harry Truman used the pool swimming while still wearing his glasses. Presidents enjoyed their leisure time swimming long before their was a pool to enjoy at the White*

House. *John Quincy Adams swam in the buff in the Potomac River while he was president. Can you imagine doing that today with YouTube and social media and paparazzo?*

4. A – Franklin D. Roosevelt

* While all the presidents listed had a part in "firsts" with a presidential limousine, it was F.D.R. who was the first to ride in an "armored" limousine. 1933, President-elect Franklin D Roosevelt had just finished giving a speech from the back of an open car when he was shot at changing history as far as the vehicle presidents would be driven in for protection. The first specially-built Presidential limousine delivered was known as the "Sunshine Special". When Pearl Harbor was attacked in December 1941, the "Sunshine Special" was still in the process of having armor plate and bulletproof windows added, and being unfinished it was unavailable. Instead, the Secret Service commandeered the bulletproof 1928 Cadillac Town Sedan that had belonged to gangster Al Capone, which had been confiscated by the IRS when Capone was arrested for tax evasion. FDR rode in Capone's car to the Capitol Building to give his "day of infamy " speech, and continued to use the "gangster car" until the Sunshine Special was completed.

** As far as the other presidents: McKinley was the first president to ride in a car. After McKinley was assassinated, Teddy Roosevelt the White House purchased their first car but Teddy preferred to ride his horse and rarely used it. William H. Taft, Roosevelt's successor, was the first to have an official presidential limousine. Woodrow Wilson was the first president to ride in a car for an official state occasion. Warren Harding was the first president to learn how to drive a car.

5. C – Dwight D. Eisenhower

6. B – Barack Obama

7. A - Lifetime security by Secret Service for presidents, wives, & children until the age of 16

* Some First Families have chosen not to have Secret Service protection even while their father is in office. The Reagan offspring are one family

that made this choice. Other First Family children have at times not liked being followed around by the Secret Service, especially those in their teens, but have realized the protection is needed – some respect that fact and others have been known to treat their Secret Service protection shabbily by trying to dodge and escape from them. The Bush twins were notorious for doing so.

8. D - Access to any movie, lifetime use of Camp David, use of Air Force 2 after retiring, gifts sent from worldwide from the time they are in office

 * *While they do have access to any movie of their choice – even those that are new releases, they do not have lifetime use of Camp David unless invited by the sitting president, Air Force 2 is for the use of the vice president and is not available to them, and gifts received during their presidency is not their property but that of the White House.*

9. B - $400,000

10. D – Designer's clothing

 * *Designers may loan some of their clothing to presidents or first ladies but they are expected to be returned. This didn't happen in the case of Nancy Reagan who kept all the gowns she had been "loaned" for state dinners that was valued well in excess of a million dollars.*

We All Have To Go Sometime:

Illness & Death

Answers are given on page 183 - 185.

1. Of the first five presidents, how many of them died on the 4th of July?

    A. 1   *C. 4*

    B. 3   *D. 2*

2. Which president suffered a stroke while president and unbeknownst to the American public was incapacitated and it was actually the First Lady who was acting as the president?

    A. James Garfield   *C. Woodrow Wilson*

    B. Franklin D. Roosevelt   *D. Warren Harding*

3. You could actually say this president's lengthy inaugural address is what killed him, since he stood in the outdoors with no hat or coat and ended up with pneumonia and died. Who was he?

    A. William H. Harrison   *C. Zachary Taylor*

    B. William McKinley   *D. John Tyler*

4. Who succeeded to the presidency after President Lincoln was assassinated?

A. Andrew Johnson   C. James Buchanan

B. Ulysses S. Grant   D. Franklin Pierce

5. Which of our presidents was in a wheelchair as a result of polio?

A. Martin Van Buren   C. Chester Arthur

B. Franklin D. Roosevelt   D. William H. Taft

6. Which president died from a heart attack while in office?

A. Woodrow Wilson   C. William H. Harrison

B. Zachary Taylor   D. Warren Harding

7. Which president was assassinated after only a few months in office?

A. James Garfield   C. William McKinley

B. Abraham Lincoln   D. John F. Kennedy

8. Which president was shot and hit twice by Lee Harvey Oswald as the president was driving by in a motorcade?

A. William McKinley   C. John F. Kennedy

B. James Garfield   D. Franklin D. Roosevelt

9. Which president had a secret operation due to cancer aboard a yacht in order to keep it a secret from the American public?

A. Grover Cleveland   C. Theodore Roosevelt

B. Rutherford B. Hayes   D. Herbert Hoover

10. Which president in his last days as he was dying was offered stimulants to keep him alive until July 4[th,] so he could join three other former presidents to have died on that historic date?

A. James Monroe   C. Thomas Jefferson

B. James Madison   D. John Adams

11. Which president survived an assassination attempt in the 1912 election, when the metal case for his glasses in his pocket stopped a bullet from going through to his heart?

A. William McKinley   C. Rutherford B. Hayes

B. William H. Taft   D. Theodore Roosevelt

12. Which president was buried at Washington National Cathedral, the only president buried in the nation's capital?

A. Harry Truman   C. Woodrow Wilson

B. John F. Kennedy   D. Chester Arthur

13. After which president was shot did Alexander Graham Bell attempt to find the bullet still inside the President by using a metal detector Bell had designed?

A. James Garfield   C. William McKinley

B. Abraham Lincoln   D. Theodore Roosevelt

14. Which two presidents died on July 4, 1826 – the 50th anniversary of the adoption of the Declaration of Independence?

    A. G. Washington & T. Jefferson   *C. J. Adams & J. Monroe*

    B. J. Adams & T. Jefferson   *D. J. Adams & J. Madison*

15. Over 50 years after his death, the American public is still not buying the story they were told that there was a single shooter in the assassination of which president?

    A. Abraham Lincoln   *C. Zachary Taylor*

    B. James Garfield   *D. John F. Kennedy*

16. Which president during his youth was saved from drowning?

    A. Ulysses S. Grant   *C. George Washington*

    B. Abraham Lincoln   *D. Donald Trump*

17. After which president's sudden death was the First Lady suspected of poisoning him?

    A. Zachary Taylor   *C. Warren Harding*

    B. William H. Harrison   *D. Franklin D. Roosevelt*

18. Which president was shot on his way to make a speech? He insisted on giving his speech before going to the hospital. The bullet was never removed.

    A. Theodore Roosevelt   *C. James Garfield*

    B. Chester Arthur   *D. Millard Fillmore*

19. Which sitting president was "assassinated" in a Shakespeare's 'Julius Caesar' play where the part of Caesar was made over to represent the president and was depicted as being brutally stabbed to death on stage?

A. James Madison

C. Barack Obama

B. Donald Trump

D. Herbert Hoover

20. Which president had two assassination attempts made on his life, both by women?

A. Ronald Reagan

C. George H.W. Bush

B. Bill Clinton

D. Gerald Ford

21. Which president requested that at his death his body be wrapped in an American flag with his head resting on a copy of the Constitution?

A. James Madison

C. Andrew Johnson

B. James Monroe

D. Abraham Lincoln

22. There was a failed assassination attempt on which president's life in the form of a car bomb in Kuwait?

A. George W. Bush

C. Ronald Reagan

B. Richard Nixon

D. George H.W. Bush

23. Which president, just two months after his inauguration, survived an assassination attempt?

A. James Garfield

C. Jimmy Carter

B. Ronald Reagan

D. George H.W. Bush

24. Who was the first president to have his funeral broadcast on the radio?

A. William McKinley

C. William H. Taft

B. Abraham Lincoln

D. Woodrow Wilson

25. Who was the first president to have an assassination attempt made on his life, but was saved because the gun did not fire properly?

A. Andrew Jackson

C. John Quincy Adams

B. James Buchanan

D. Martin Van Buren

26. As a teen, what president underwent major surgery and was given only brandy as a sedative?

A. James Polk

C. William H. Harrison

B. John Tyler

D. Ulysses S. Grant

27. Which president, just a year after becoming president, learned he had a fatal kidney disease?

A. James Polk

C. Benjamin Harrison

B. Chester Arthur

D. Warren Harding

28. It was revealed after which president's retirement that he had Alzheimer's disease. Who was he?

A. George W. Bush

C. Bill Clinton

B. Ronald Reagan

D. Jimmy Carter

29. How many presidents have been assassinated?

    A. 6   *C. 3*

    B. 5   *D. 4*

30. After an assassination attempt was made on this president's life, on the way to surgery to remove the bullet he jokingly said, "I forgot to duck." Who is he?

    A. George W. Bush   *C. Ronald Reagan*

    B. Barack Obama   *D. Calvin Coolidge*

Answers

Chapter 20 – We All Have To Go Sometime: Illness & Death

1. B - 3

John Adams and Thomas Jefferson both died on July 4th, 1826 and James Monroe died on July 4th, 1831.

2. C - Woodrow Wilson

3. A - William H. Harrison

4. A - Andrew Johnson

5. B - Franklin D. Roosevelt

6. D - Warren Harding

It is believed he died of a heart attack though some suspected the First Lady of poisoning the president. No autopsy was preformed at her request and he was cremated within 24 hours of his death.

7. A - James Garfield

8. C - John F. Kennedy

Though still to this day, many question the fact of who actually shot and killed the president making this one of the longest, ongoing conspiracy theories in American history.

9. A - Grover Cleveland

10. B - James Madison

He refused.

11. D - Theodore Roosevelt

12. C - Woodrow Wilson

While Arlington National Cemetery is just across the Potomac River, it lies in the state of Virginia.

13. A - James Garfield

Unfortunately, he was unsuccessful in locating the bullet due to the doctors limiting the area he could search. The president died from infection and internal hemorrhaging.

14. B - John Adams and Thomas Jefferson

15. D - John F. Kennedy

16. A - Ulysses S. Grant

17. C - Warren Harding

18. A - Theodore Roosevelt

19. B - Donald Trump

20. D - Gerald Ford

21. C - Andrew Johnson

22. D - George H.W. Bush

23. B - Ronald Reagan

24. C - William H. Taft

25. A - Andrew Jackson

26. A - James Polk

27. B - Chester Arthur

28. B - Ronald Reagan

29. D - 4

Abraham Lincoln, James Garfield, William McKinley, and John F. Kennedy

30. C - Ronald Reagan

www.ingramcontent.com/pod-product-compliance
Lightning Source LLC
LaVergne TN
LVHW051053080426
835508LV00019B/1848